CW00544269

COLOURS OF THE CUT

Edward Paget-Tomlinson

Element's day boat loaded with coal for Wolverhampton, near Curdworth, July 1955.

Left: Gauging the draught of a F. M. & C. butty at Brentford. Right: Joe Tolley aboard *Dragon* at Ellesmere Port, 1940s.
Opposite page and colour illustration above: See pages 56-59

COLOURS OF THE CUT

THE COMPANY COLOURS OF THE INLAND WATERWAY WORKING BOATS OF BRITAIN

Edward Paget-Tomlinson

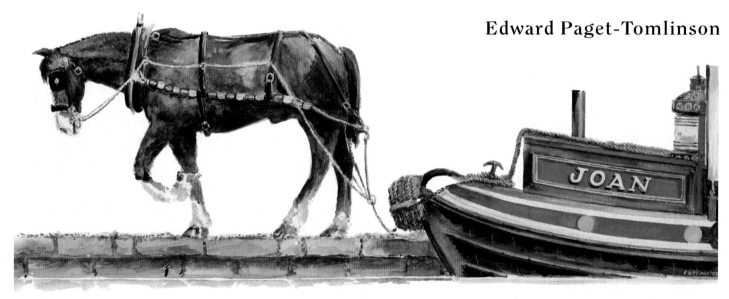

Landmark Publishing

Above left: Pairs of narrow boats waiting for orders at Sutton Stop, near Coventry, in May 1962.

Above right: Leeds & Liverpool 'long' boat transom stern, Litherland, 1940s

Bottom left: River Weaver 'packet' *Caledonia* leaving Hunts Lock, Northwich, 1957.

Bottom right: British Waterways' butty *Raven* leaving top lock, Audlem, September 1957.

Craft illustrated in colour indexed by name and by company

A Crook & Thompson motor short boat at Johnson's Hillock, 1962.

In 1987 Hugh Potter, the editor of the monthly *Waterways World* magazine, asked me to consider producing a short series of pictures of narrow canal boats painted in their historic company colours, loaded with appropriate cargoes. They were to be perspective views and were to go inside the back cover to succeed a feature called 'Canals in Colour', full page photographs of recent scenes up and down the system. For the new series a set of new paintings was suggested as colour photographs were unlikely to be available of older craft, and, as water colours do not reproduce with sufficient strength, gouache paint was chosen, the opaque design colour of school art classes. I tried a perspective view of a Cowburn & Cowpar horse boat but it turned out poorly, not at all what the editor wanted. Sending me a page from an aircraft magazine displaying side elevations of jet fighters in colour with their markings and insignia, he asked if narrow boats could be similarly treated. They could, I replied, but to show colours and decoration to advantage there would only be room on the page for the cabin and stern with no real indication of the cargo. A Shropshire Union boat, the *Elector*, was drawn with greater success and paired with the stern of a Midlands and Coast boat the *Orion* to appear in the November 1987 *Waterways World* under the title 'Colours of the Cut No 1: On the Shroppie'.

This new inside back cover feature was well received and seven more sets of 'Colours' were proposed and prepared - Fellows Morton & Clayton, Cowburn & Cowpar and Thomas Clayton, the Grand Union Canal Carrying Co Ltd, the Anderton and Mersey-Weaver companies, Cadbury's, Severn & Canal, Ovaltine and Samuel Barlow, British Waterways and Willow Wren, this last in the June 1988 issue. But it was certainly not to be the last as by this time reader reaction was enthusiastic and there was a demand for more. More could be provided - so far I had only touched the tip of the iceberg and soon after came a B.C.N. set, Potter's of Runcorn, Seddon's of Middlewich, Peate's the Oswestry millers, Harvey-Taylor of Aylesbury, L. B. Faulkner of Leighton Buzzard and so on. No terminal date was suggested - the series would end when we ran out of colours. From the start a short text went with the pictures which became longer and more informative as the series advanced. It always includes a spate of acknowledgements which are grouped together in this book.

It is invidious to single out names but early contact was made with the then unopened National Waterways Museum at Gloucester and David McDougall of the curatorial team was very helpful; painting specifications for the first Grand Union livery were found, and for Cowburn & Cowpar, and many photographs were produced. At the Gloucester museum the series provided inspiration for a display of cabin sides of giant proportions, drawn to one-eighth full size but enlarged to one-quarter and then reduced to provide a set of postcards. One vital need was a boat's registration number and any gauging numbers she may have carried. Here Alan Faulkner has provided richly without omission from Runcorn to Basingstoke. The registration number gives a clue to the date of build and to alterations of ownership, so a history can be prepared. Without Alan's continuous assistance the series would have been much less successful and this book owes him a big debt as well. To attempt to record the correct colours, help has been sought and freely given from Sheffield to Sharpness, but sadly some of the helpers have passed on since the series started. This emphasizes the last minute nature of much of the information – delay could have meant irretrievable loss. Inevitably much has been lost in any case, although tonal interpretation of black and white photographs has become a fine art. It could be said 'put what you think, nobody is likely to contradict you', but this is unethical to an historian; once published the 'Colours' would become a work of reference and errors become the truth. If there is doubt the caption must say so. Of course there have been mistakes and I have been pleased to learn them and print the correction in *Waterways World*.

As the series progressed people wondered how long it could continue, but the narrow boat colours kept coming, the B.C.N. providing a rich harvest except that most of the carriers and steerers favoured red cabin sides with a green border. Readers, including the editor of *Waterways World* were cutting out the back cover and pasting it up, and many turned to the inside back cover as soon as the magazine arrived. The *Waterways World* opinion poll was favourable, artists were grateful for the information, boat owners wrote in asking for the colours their craft originally wore, others commissioned pictures of their craft, notably B.C.N. tug owners, and the National Waterways Museum at Gloucester reported more enquiries about colour schemes. *Waterways World* produced calendars with them in 1990, 1991, 1993 and 1994, and discussions about a book of the series were started following reader demand.

In the summer of 1989 the Inland Waterways Association National Rally was held at Waltham Abbey on the Lea and to tie in with this 'Colours of the Cut No 23' featured an explosives barge, the *Lady of the Lea* built in 1931 for the War Department traffic from the Royal Gunpowder Factory at Waltham Abbey. Suddenly the narrow boat sequence was broken and other craft could be introduced which increased the scope and probable length of the series. November saw Leeds and Liverpool boats, January 1990 flats and keels from the Rochdale, whilst later that year came Yorkshire keels and sloops, Severn tugs and Weaver packets. Narrow boats were now alternating with other types, some not so colourful such as Severn trows and some a bit marginal like Thames spritsail barges. Scotland, Ireland and South Wales were not forgotten and the series moved on to include not only colour but the range of craft which have used and are using all the inland waterways, from the Norfolk Broads to the Shannon, from the Forth and Clyde to the Parrett. In this book some extra craft have been worked in, illustrations that were prepared for particular articles, a double page spread in June 1989 to mark the Fellows, Morton and Clayton centenary, and in June 1991 an extra Norfolk wherry, the *Spray*. Sometimes it was possible to tie in a 'Colour' with an article, a current event or a rally and this became policy, for instance the 'Back of the Map' boats in September 1991 to coincide with the I.W.A. National Rally at Windmill End on the Dudley. With non- narrow boats it has generally been possible to draw the whole craft, although sailing vessels appear a bit small. I would say as the artist that I have learnt much from practice and some of the early efforts do not look so good now. I must admit that narrow boat cabin sides have come off best. Everything was drawn to twice reproduction size, which means generous detail for cans, pigeon boxes and castles, whereas at only twice the finished size the rigging of a Humber keel remains finicky and confusing.

Edward Paget-Tomlinson,
Wells, Somerset.

A Second Introduction

The paragraphs above were written by Edward some time in the mid-1990s for a version of this book which did not finally come to fruition. As he indicates the idea of publishing the 'Colours of the Cut' as one book was in place even before the full sequence of 80 consecutive numbers was completed in June 1994. Unfortunately it has taken another ten years to bring that plan to fruition. In the meantime, sadly, we have lost Edward himself for he died in November 2003 from complications following surgery for cancer, a great loss to all who knew him and the world of waterways in general. However his plans for this book were well underway and it has been a sad but satisfactory task for his widow Pam and I to try and complete this last unfinished project as he would have wished. It is the culmination of a huge body of work – research, books, articles, paintings and illustrations – and all of this on top of an already distinguished career in museums.

Because the paintings were not originally seen as forming any sort of connective narrative, Edward wrote each original caption to stand alone for that month, sometimes with topical references to that particular edition of the magazine. However as a book, with pages

Portrait of the author, Edward Paget-Tomlinson, at Atherstone in 1962.

that are likely to be read consecutively, both illustrations and captions needed to hold together in some sort of logical progression. Edward had already sorted out another preferred sequence of pictures so we have been able to follow his visual progression of ideas fairly closely. However, because of this change of format, including a number of rearrangements of pictures on the page, few of the original captions have been retained. Happily Edward had also already rewritten most of them to include masses more historical detail. Some were almost articles in themselves, a few of which I have had to edit somewhat to keep the pages manageable. I have had to add to some of the captions because there are a number of paintings included here that were prepared as illustrations to articles in the magazine, and in each of these I have usually abstracted information from the articles they accompanied:

Midland Carriers pages 22/23 is from Alan Faulkner's article about T.& S. Element, WW September 1996;
Spray of Norwich pages 146/147 from Nigel Royall's article 'A Norwich Waterman' WW June 1991;
Stover Canal pages 154/155 is from Marilyn Hunter's article about the Stover Canal, WW May 1999.

Edward's basic information for compiling this pictorial catalogue of canal craft liveries came mainly from his own research, careful notes of conversations stretching back to his own discovery of the canal world in the 1950s when he was working at the National Maritime Museum at Greenwich. Edward particularly acknowledged the influence of Commander H. Oliver Hill who became something of a mentor to the young museum assistant at the time, encouraging him to take a careful historical interest in the humble craft of the inland waterways as well as in the grander ships of the high seas, an interest that gradually became the core of his research for the following fifty years.

All the following names are thanked and credited in the original captions to the magazine entries, many of them several times over of course, but I hope those individuals will not mind just a single mention here, for brevity. Edward was grateful, and Pam and I are very pleased to be able to acknowledge them all once again. Thank you Tommy Appleton, Harry Arnold, Dan Ashcroft, Reg Barnett, Ian Bath, Harry and Sarah Bentley, Malcolm Braine, Malcolm Bristow, Cadbury's Ltd, Mike Clarke, Hugh Compton, Euan Corrie, Pat Crecraft, J. B. Dalton, Richard Dean, Ruth Delaney, Mr Ellis of Widnes, Peter Ferguson, Kenneth Formby of Rugby Portland Cement, Tom Foxon, John Frank, John Gibbons, John Gould, Fred Greenham, John and James Griffin, Kevin Griffin, Clive Guthrie, W. A. (Tony) Harmsworth, Fred Higgins, Dave and Jennifer Hilton, Roger Hipkiss, Alan Holden, Bob Keaveney, Ian Kemp, Andrew King, Sir John Knill, James Lawson, Bill Leathwood, Tim Lewis, Robert Malster, Christopher March, Beryl McDowell, Brian J. Murless, Patricia O'Driscoll, Joe Palin, J. G. Parkinson, Jim Pedan, Tom Prendegast, Paul Proud, L. G. Reid, Alan Roberts, Frank Rogers, Kenneth Roseblade, Michael Sampson, Don Sattin, John Saxon, Alan Scarth of Merseyside Maritime Museum, Fred Schofield, R. J. Scott, Alan Smith, Phil Speight, Mike Stammers, Mike Sumner, Geoff Taylor, Mike Taylor, Harry Theobalds, Mike and Cath Turpin, John Vickers, Dr Charles Waine, Anthony J. Walker, Peter Walsh, A. Wander Ltd, Warwickshire Fly Boat Co, Philip Watkinson, Mike Webb, Steve White, Graham Wigley, Michael Wildey, Robert Wilson, Elizabeth and David Wood, Herbert and Betty Wood, Reg Wood, Joe Worsey, Ian L. Wright, Sam Yates, Tim and Andy Young.

Three other names do re-occur so often in Edward's credit lists that they each deserve some extra comment. The late Ken Keay is the first, a boatbuilder and canal carrier from Walsall in the Midlands. They met soon after Edward bought the Thos. Clayton tar boat *Gifford* for restoration in 1970, initially just as a business arrangement but it blossomed into a long and fruitful friendship. Although increasing interest was being shown by then in the art and culture of the long distance narrow boat, the fleets of simple straight stemmed open boats of the B.C.N. were seen as rather poor relations, and their importance was in danger of being forgotten. Ken was very concerned about this for these boats had been his life's work, and his father's before him, so he was particularly pleased to make Edward's acquaintance. Here was an academic canal historian taking a serious professional interest in the region's 'joey' boats at last, for Edward was by then working on his monumental canal encyclopaedia. It is perhaps an indication of the importance that he accorded the Birmingham boats and Ken's information that when he re-arranged the magazine series for book publication he chose to start with the simple 'joey' boats of Wolverhampton and

Pair of British Waterways' boats working south through Fishery Lock on the Grand Union, April 1956.

the Black Country. Ken's knowledge had been crucial to all these entries.

David McDougall and Alan Faulkner are both acknowledged in Edward's own paragraphs but it was only whilst checking through the original magazine captions for this publication that we realised just how often their names were acknowledged, time after time. Both are perfectionists in their fields and their painstaking help and encouragement was much appreciated by Edward, and we are indebted to them as well.

This book has offered the opportunity to publish some relevant photographs alongside the paintings. Many of them are Edward's own pictures, adequate proof that among all his other talents he was also a very competent photographer. Most of the other prints were in his own research collection, a few of them the prime source of the information for the paintings, whilst a dozen or so have been specifically researched from the archive collection at the Boat Museum, Ellesmere Port. We have managed to contact the majority of the owners of the originals for their permission to reproduce them here, but inevitably a number of contacts have been lost over the years, and we beg the forgiveness of any of the owners or their descendants who we have not been able to contact directly. Please accept our apologies and thanks, and we hope you approve the use to which they have been put.

Thank you to all of the following people and organisations for the use of their photographs: Enoch Appleton 34; Harry Arnold/Waterway Images 56, 84a, 92a, 92b, 164b; Sarah Bentley 42a; Gordon Biddle coll. 132a, 132b; Admiral Blake Museum, Bridgwater 154; Robert Buddle 124a; Cadbury Bros. 62, 64 left; Cheshire & Chester Archives and Local Studies 72b, 88, 116b; Mike Clarke 66a; Leslie Cooke 22, 76b; Euan Corrie 116a; Richard J. Dean 7, 96; Grahame E. Farr 158 left; Eddie Frangleton 84b; Gainsborough Library 142; Arthur Guinness & Co. 174; Fred Higgins 114a; Commander H. O. Hill 70, 121, 136a, 152a, 152b, 162a, 162b;

John Hill 10; Jim Hollingshead 28b; Graham Hovey 30; Selwyn Jordan 58 right, 90b; Ken Keay 16 left, 20, 108b, 112a, 112b; Will King coll.16 right; Dave Kitchin coll. 124b; Mike LeRoy 28a; Tony Lewery coll. 24a, 38a, 50 left, 78b, 94, 104, 122 right, 144, 147, 156 left, 158 right; Merseyside County Museums 126, 164a; Peter Norton 140a, 166; Barbara Nurser 36; Jack Parkinson 1, 11a, 24b, 26a, 26b, 42b, 58 left, 74, 80b, 108a, 110a, 128a, 128b, 130b; P. L. Smith 140b; Geoff Taylor 76a; Harry Theobalds 90a; Betty Thorpe 44; Leah Tolley 2 right; The Waterways Trust (Archive collections at Gloucester and Ellesmere Port) 18 left, 32, 38b, 46, 48a, 48b, 54a, 54b, 64 right, 78a, 86a, 82, 98, 100, 102, 106, 110b, 114b, 122 left, 148, 150, 160; Michael Ware coll. 86b; Philip Watkinson 4 upper right, 130a; Robert Wilson coll. 60a, 60b, 72a, 80a; Reginald Wood 15, 138, 170.

All other unaccredited photos are by the author, or are from his collection.

This book seems to be an apt place for Edward's work to stop for these paintings sum up so much of what he loved about the waterways and the culture that grew up on them. The colour schemes and richness of decoration on inland boats and barges can stand as symbols of something much bigger than a bit of cheerfulness, reflecting an attitude to the working boats by those who worked in the canal world – the boat men and women, the boat builders and painters. The paintwork spoke of a pride in the trade and a care for the tools of the trade, a place where art became inextricably tangled up with the everyday working life of the boat population. It was only a few pots of paint but their use had an importance quite out of proportion to the simplicity of the idea. Well-designed boats did a simple transport job with grace and dignity. With colour they did it with a quite unnecessary added beauty that reminds us that we are human, and can be quite nice.

Tony Lewery, Ellesmere, Shropshire. July 2004

Bibliography

It is not practical to offer a full bibliography here of all the publications relevant to Edward's research because it would be so immense as to be rather meaningless, needing to cover almost every title ever published about canals and waterways. However he did mention several publications by name in his acknowledgements to specific 'Colours of the Cut' entries and it is proper that they should be listed here. The references are mainly to photographs included in them:

Tom Chaplin, *The Narrow Boat Book*, 1978 (Fore Cabins)
Roy Clark, *Black Sailed Traders*, 1961 (Norfolk Wherries)
K. R. Clew, *History of the Kennet and Avon*, (K. & A. Carriers)
Hugh Conway-Jones, *History of Gloucester Docks*, 1984 (Salt Union)
Michael T. Greenwood, *Rochdale Canal*, (Rochdale Boats)
Charles Hadfield and Gordon Biddle, *Canals of North West England*, 1970 (Lancaster Canal)
Peter Lead, *The Trent and Mersey Canal*, 1980 (Salt Union)
A. J. Lewery, *Narrow Boat Painting*, 1974
Tony Lewery, *Flowers Afloat*, 1996
Robert Malster, *Wherries & Waterways*, 1986 (Norfolk Wherries)
Dan McDonald, *The Clyde Puffer*, 1977 (Puffers)
J. E. G. McKee, *Working Boats of Britain*, 1983 (Bridgwater & Taunton)
P. A. L. Vine, *London's Lost Route to Basingstoke*, 1968 (On the Basingstoke)
A. J. Walker, *Walker's of Ricky*, 1991
Michael Ware, *Narrow Boats at Work*, 1980 (Maintenance Boats)
C. P. & C. R. Weaver, *Steam on Canals*, 1983 (Sand and Cement)
Ian L. Wright, *Canals in Wales*, 1977 (Maintenance Boats)

Rega OLDBURY No 19

T & S. ELEMENT
— LIMITED —

MAYS FLOWER

For T. & S. Element information see pages 22 & 23

Other books by Edward Paget-Tomlinson:

Instruments of Navigation A catalogue of the navigational instruments in the National Maritime Museum, with Commander H. O. Hill. 1953
History of the Bibby Line pub. Bibby Line. 1969 & 1982
Mersey & Weaver Flats pub. Robert Wilson 1973
Canal & River Navigations pub. Waine Research 1978
Britain's Canal & River Craft pub. Moorland Publishing 1979
The Montreux-Oberland Bernois Railway pub. M.O.B. 1984
The Railway Carriers pub. Terence Dalton Ltd., 1990
An Illustrated History of Canal & River Navigations pub. Sheffield Academic Press 1993
Waterways in the Making pub. Landscape Press 1996

In addition it should be noted that Edward created many detailed illustrations for other author's works as well. Of particular relevance to the subject of this book are:

Corrie, Euan, *Tales from the Old Inland Waterways* pub. David & Charles 1998
Faulkner, Alan, *The Grand Junction Canal* pub. W. H. Walker & Bros. 1993
Pellow, Thomas, *Waterways at Work* pub. The Landscape Press 2000
Schofield, Fred, *Humber Keels and Keelmen* pub. Terence Dalton Ltd. 1988
Stammers, Mike, *Mersey Flats and Flatmen* pub. Terence Dalton Ltd. 1993
Walker, Anthony J., *Walkers' of Ricky* pub. W. H. Walker & Bros. 1991

Albert Wood of Sowerby Bridge had Mersey flats on the Rochdale Canal and keels on the Calder & Hebble plus a few narrow boats based on Manchester, mainly working on the Ashton and Peak Forest canals. His son Reg, to whom I am indebted for a great deal of canal information, has made models of the flats and two of the narrow boats, the *Nymph* and the *Ceres* and evidence of the colours comes from these. They were not highly decorated, the predominating yellow being inherited from the Rochdale carrier William Jackson, two of whose boats Albert Wood bought in 1894 to start his own business. I am afraid the registration number of the *Nymph* is fictitious; research has not revealed the correct one.

An Albert Wood owned Calder & Hebble keel at Shepley Bridge dockyard, 1911.

Birmingham Canal Navigations

Traffic on the Birmingham and Black Country canals was handled by quite a variety of craft but their common factor was that they were day boats and were never lived in continuously. Many were open boats without shelter of any kind, including those running to the canal/rail interchange stations. They were built on the lines of long distance boats with a rounded stem, a fine entry and a well-raked stern. Indeed they were called 'round stemmed boats' or 'station boats'

on the cut. One of these is illustrated here, British Rail's London Midland Region *No 22*, built of steel, which was at work into the 1950s. She was descended from the Shropshire Union fly-boats which carried on behalf of the London & North Western Railway. The L.N.W.R., L.M.S. and B.R. continued where the S.U. left off and it is thought the old colours were kept. (see page 107)

Most B.C.N. boats however were more primitive, with stem and stern identical, (the definition of a 'joey boat') with vertical stemposts with no flare at either end. For speed it was normal not to turn these boats round (not to 'wind' them in canal parlance), because they were truly double-ended and the rudders would be transferred from boat to boat, and could be hung on either end. They had their own decorative tradition with the emphasis on rapid recognition, because steerers moved from boat to boat. Owners needed distinctive symbols to identify their boats, while helms had the initials or name of the owners or the steerage company carved into the stock.

Although cabinless boats were common, with decoration limited to the shoulders at each end, there were plenty of day boats with cabins, although never so long or elaborate as those of long distance boats. Red and green were the preferred cabin side colours and the

Charles shown here was a typical example. She was built by Peter Keay & Son at their Pratt's Bridge Dock, Walsall, just before the Second World War for the Aston coal merchants Charles Williams. Keay's recorded their docking date within a string of diamonds down the cabin waterway, K for Keay then the completion day, month and year thus: K-1-6-40. In 1936 Peter Keay converted the Shropshire Union horse boat *Wilden* into a 70 ft motor tug, fitting

Above right: Railway interchange boat near Netherton tunnel, about 1952.
Above left: *The Dart* with Ken Keay at the tiller, about 1940.

a counter and named her *The Dart*. Ken, Peter's son, was the dock painter, and these two boats illustrate his style of decoration. One of his 'trademarks' was the stylised eight-petalled flower on the engine hole and cabin doors.

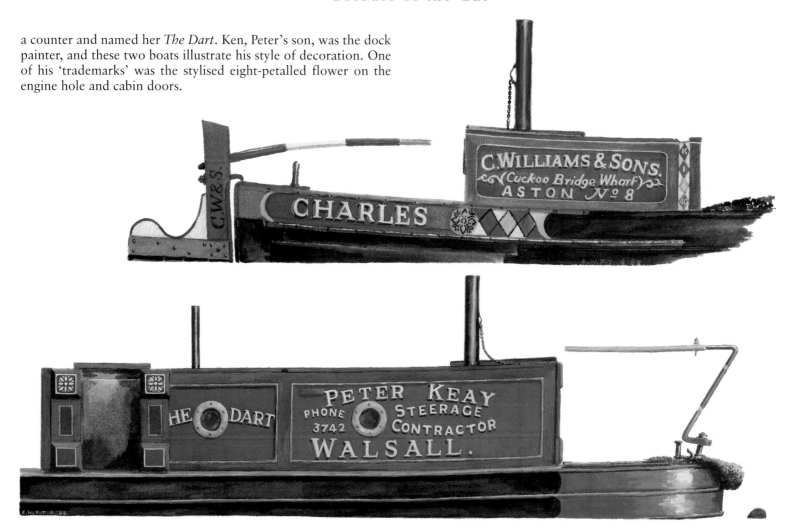

Light Boats

So called by the Black Country boatmen, 'light' boats carried coal to power stations. Electric power generating stations were built by the canals not only to solve steam condensing problems but to receive coal by boat – Birchills, Ocker Hill and Nechells, near Salford Junction were examples, as was Stourport power station opened in 1926 and served by the Staffs and Worcester Canal. This was built by the Shropshire, Worcestershire & Staffordshire Electric Power Company, based at Smethwick, who acquired their first boat in 1915.

Their early fleet was all second hand, numbered not named, and came from a variety of sources: Severn & Canal, Albright & Wilson and Thomas Element. From the mid-1920s new boats appeared, with electrical names like *Ampic* and *Wattic* which were among those built by Peter Keay at Daw End to bring Cannock Chase coal to Stourport. The *James* was a later arrival, built by Peter Keay at Walsall in 1938 and subsequently docked by him. She was named after Jimmy Stansfield, the power company's 'outrider' or manager.

Above left: Nechells power station, Birmingham, with at least 20 B.C.N.coal boats waiting to unload in the 1930s.

Above right: B.E.A. coal boat at work, with Keay's docking date marked on the watercourse, about 1950.

No 24 is an earlier boat docked by Peter Keay at Daw End as the date on the cabin side watercourse shows. Because 1935 was the Silver Jubilee year of King George V and Queen Mary the company temporarily adopted a red, white and blue colour scheme.

Electrical power companies were nationalised on the 1 April 1948 and the S.W.& S.E.P. Co. became part of the British Electricity Authority. Their *Andrew* had been built by Peter Keay at Walsall in 1938 and was named after Captain Andrew Hastie, one of the power company's hierarchy. She too went to Keay's for docking. In 1954 the B.E.A. became the Central Electricity Authority avoiding confusion with British European Airways, and C.E.A. appeared on the boats. Local power station traffic ceased in 1965.

Considering the grimy cargoes and rough usage it is surprising how much decoration was applied to these B.C.N. boats. Shoulder and cabin side decoration was essential for rapid recognition because it was the usual practice for the steerer to deliver one boat and immediately transfer the stove, helm and towing mast to another for the return trip. Thus the diamonds, roundels and crescent moons on the shoulders and the distinctive patterns on the boards of the cabin back which tended to be adopted as trademarks of the various boat docks. Here are three examples of Ken Keay's decorative work at Peter Keay & Son's dock, first at Daw End, then at Pratt's Bridge, Walsall. Red, white and green were the favourite colours, red shoulders with a white surround, a green false guard and sometimes a run of diamonds in contrasting colours under the cabin. Cabin sides were mostly red, bordered by green with a white dividing line and white or off-white lettering heavily shaded in light and dark green, or blue and black. There were exceptions like the Lawrence Miller boat shown here, built in 1914 before Peter Keay started his business, but he did dock her. Miller had a fleet of twenty or so delivering factory coal in Birmingham. They were based at Cambrian Wharf, Birmingham with the offices in Martineau Street.

Hickenbotham's was another with their red diamond set in blue. The *Betty* was a wharf boat delivered by Peter Keay & Son at Walsall in 1933, the only wharf boat they built, 86ft long by 8ft 4in beam with a capacity of 49½ tons of coal. She worked the lock-free level between Anglesey Basin at the end of the Cannock extension and factories in the Ocker Hill and Bradley area for Thomas Hickenbotham & Sons of Wednesbury, coal merchants, abbreviated on the cabin side and rudder to T.H.& S.W. Many owners limited their titles to initials, S.S.S., E.A.R. etc., easily

The newly painted *Joan & Doreen* on dock at Pratts Bridge, Walsall, in the early 1930s with the painter Ken Keay standing in the hold.

spotted and memorised but one or two companies went to greater symbolic lengths. Johnson's Iron & Steel of West Bromwich had the eye, presumably of the Cyclops, whilst Samuel Pearson the bottle maker had a bottle on the bow.

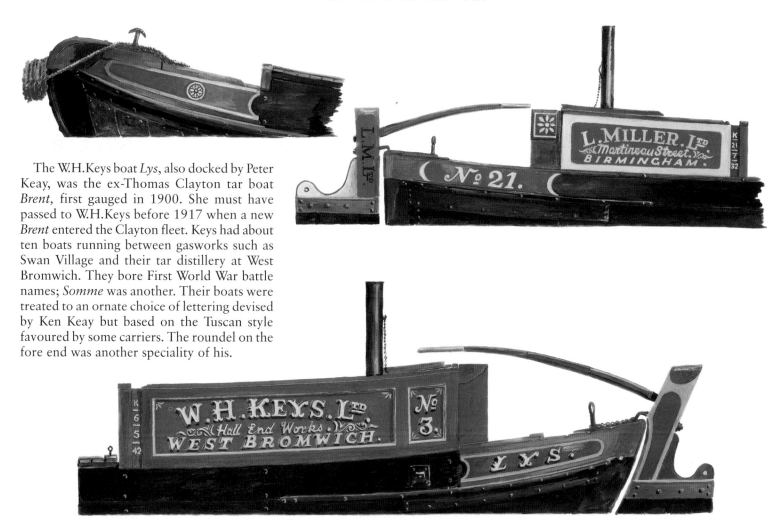

The W.H.Keys boat *Lys*, also docked by Peter Keay, was the ex-Thomas Clayton tar boat *Brent*, first gauged in 1900. She must have passed to W.H.Keys before 1917 when a new *Brent* entered the Clayton fleet. Keys had about ten boats running between gasworks such as Swan Village and their tar distillery at West Bromwich. They bore First World War battle names; *Somme* was another. Their boats were treated to an ornate choice of lettering devised by Ken Keay but based on the Tuscan style favoured by some carriers. The roundel on the fore end was another speciality of his.

T. & S. Element was started by the brothers Thomas and Samuel back in the 1890s. The company expanded dramatically in the 1920s and their two hundred or so boats remained busy until after the Second World War, concentrating on coal traffic. They did introduce several motor boats and tugs to the fleet latterly but they continued to operate horse boats right through to the end of the canal carrying contracts, running from their own stable yard and boat dock at Salford Bridge until the M6 motorway was constructed through the site. The day boat *Sapphire*, typical of the large number of such craft in Elements' fleet, was built by Yates Bros. at Norton Canes in 1954. She was one of the last craft to enter service and lasted until 1977, being one of those docked by Peter Keay & Son at Walsall. *Sapphire* eventually became part of the Boat Museum collection at Ellesmere Port where she awaits restoration.

Midlands & Coast Canal Carriers was one of the companies set up to take over some of the traffic after the demise of the Shropshire Union Railways & Canal Company in 1921. (see page 112) Although they had their own boat dock at Old Hill they also had their boats docked elsewhere, including Keay's yard at Walsall where Ken Keay remembered docking the *Orion*, a boat built by William Nurser at Braunston in 1922, and eventually sold on to T.&S. Element in 1941. Ken was able to advise the Black Country Museum at Dudley when they restored the Midland & Coast's *Diamond*, which is on display on their slipway exhibition.

Midland & Coast boats on their own dock at Old Hill on the Dudley Canal.

Knobsticks

Among the major carriers of the North West and a main carrier on the Trent & Mersey Canal with at one time as many as 200 narrow boats, the Anderton Company had a history going back to the early nineteenth century as Alexander Reid & Co. They started as general carriers but from 1829 were specialising in the carriage of pottery raw materials and finished ware packed in crates, transhipping both cargoes to river flats at Anderton where the Weaver runs fifty feet below the canal. So much of their business became concentrated there that in 1836 Reid's retitled themselves as the Anderton Company. But they ran into financial difficulty and in 1848 were bought by the Bridgewater Trustees who were protecting their traffic by buying the carrying companies which fed them. They in turn were acquired by railway interests and in 1876 the Anderton Company was sold to William Boddington and Edward Pamphilon who retained the Bridgewater agency and had to state this on the cabin sides of their boats. The *Thames* pictured here was built in 1902 most probably at Runcorn for she was registered there; from May 1912 all boats were registered at Stoke when the company

Anderton Co. boat *Batavia* alongside Meakin's *Scotia* in Runcorn Docks, about 1910.

Motor *Walton* with butty *Darlaston* crewed by Mr and Mrs Evans leaving the Anderton lift in March 1956.

opened the dock at Middleport which replaced the old one at Anderton. Their boats were of distinctive design because of the crated pottery they carried down to the Mersey, all wood with fine lines fore and aft so that they swam especially well. For some unclear reason they were called 'knobstick' boats and their crews 'knobstick' men, perhaps originating from patrolmen on the Trent & Mersey who carried some sort of baton of office. The first known colour scheme was simple and striking, black and white with yellow shaded white lettering. The naming was delightfully varied – rivers, countries, girls' names, planets and such names as *Celtic* and *Cymric* like the White Star liners.

Motor boats entered the fleet from 1923 when the horse boat *Westminster* was converted at Faulkner's dock at Leighton Buzzard. More were added, both converted and built new and by 1940 there were sixteen, all with Bolinder engines. The company contracted in the 1940s, the final six motors and seven butties being bought by

the Mersey-Weaver Co. in 1953. (see page 26) The sale included the *Denmark* a motor built at Middleport in 1929. The new owners allowed the Anderton colours and title to remain but by this time they had changed to a black and yellow scheme, with 'Bridgewater Navigation Route' removed. Eventually on 1 February 1958 the combined fleets passed to British Waterways.

Parallel with the Anderton Company history went that of the younger competitor that finally took them over. Mersey Weavers was a child of the Winsford salt producers who, expecting an expansion of general traffic to the Middlewich branch of the Shropshire Union, had founded the Weaver & Mersey Carrying Co. in 1864. However, the formation of the Salt Union in 1888 brought all the salt firms together along with their varied craft including those of the Weaver & Mersey Co. (see page 33 and 169) Rationalisation was needed and in 1894, the year the Manchester Ship Canal was opened, the subsidiary Mersey, Weaver & Ship Canal Carrying Co. Ltd. was formed. It concentrated mainly on the narrow boat traffic to and from the Potteries, raw materials up and crated ware returning to Anderton. Here there were crate hoists and the company had a transhipment depot. The main office was at Burslem however, and they had their own boat dock on the Burslem arm.

In 1937 Salt Union sold Mersey Weavers to its manager Charles W. Shirley. He acquired not only the general carrying fleet but the Salt Union's own narrow boats in the salt trade in Cheshire, handed over by the parent company back in the 1920s. The boats were a

Evelyn towing her butty *Florence* along the Bridgewater Canal near Broadheath in 1956 with Mrs Barnett at the tiller.

mixed crowd, mostly second hand, some from Cowburn & Cowpar, and some from A.& A. Peate of Oswestry. There were few new ones although they built the butty *Cuthbert* themselves in 1937. Mersey Weavers' first motor boat was the *Walton* built by Fellows, Morton & Clayton at Uxbridge in 1937, followed by the *Empire* converted from a horse boat in 1941. Thereafter motor boats were built at their Longport dock, ten of them eventually. Expansion came in 1953 when Leslie Shirley, Charles' son bought the by now small Anderton Company from the Boddington family along with their more up-to-date Middleport dock which was then shared by both fleets. The Longport dock closed. Two final boats came from John Green of Macclesfield in 1955 but the whole fleet passed to British Waterways in 1958. They were all wooden boats and in fairly run-down condition by that time, known disparagingly as 'watercress beds', and were soon taken out of service and sunk out of the way.

The first colour scheme was black and white with green beading, similar to that of the Salt Union. In fact *Foxland* was an old Salt Union boat built in 1901. She came to Mersey Weavers in 1924 and went on to the L.M.S. in 1945. The motor boat *Charles* was built in 1942 at the Longport dock and was named after the elder Mr Shirley. By this time a red and green colour scheme had been

Motor boat *Charles* reversing into the top lock at Hulme, Manchester in 1959 before the three locks were converted into one deep one.

adopted and 'Weaver Route', meaning via the Anderton Lift, had been erased in favour of 'General Carriers'. Naming was mixed, rivers inherited from the Salt Union, countries, flowers, boys and girls first names while the Peate's boats brought some old Shropshire Union names.

Pots and Potters

These two companies were well known on the Trent & Mersey Canal and both specialised in pottery materials. Potter's were a Runcorn firm which started carrying in the 1870s, taking clay, flint, feldspar and further raw materials up to the Potteries from ships in Weston Point and Runcorn docks, returning with coal and crated pots for export. By the 1920s they are known to have had up to thirty boats, all wooden and all horse drawn. No motors were acquired until 1948 when four came from the Anderton Company. *Sunlight* was built in 1939 and was latterly paired with the motor *Silver Jubilee* so named to commemorate the Silver Wedding Anniversary of King George VI and Queen Elizabeth in 1948. These two were the last Potter's boats to trade and were finally sold in 1958 to Peter Keay & Son of Walsall. All their boat names began with the letter S and included a bird series – *Seagull* etc. and a sun series – *Sunbeam* etc.

Potters, along with a number of other smaller companies, docked their boats at the Anderton Company dock at Middleport where, from the 1930s, William Hodgson was employed as the full time signwriter and decorator. He developed a very elaborate and characteristic style of the traditional 'roses and castles' of the narrow boats which was very popular with the Cheshire boatmen of the Trent & Mersey, a specifically 'knobstick' style of painting that was much admired and copied. A typical Hodgson castle appears on the cabin side of the *Sunlight*.

J. & G. Meakin Ltd., proprietors of the Eagle pottery at Hanley had a small fleet of no more than three horse boats running raw materials up from the docks and crated ware back to Runcorn. In 1944 they had the *Alice* converted to a motor boat and she latterly worked alone until they gave up canal transport in 1953. The docking of this small fleet was also entrusted to the Anderton Company, so again William Hodgson was responsible for the decoration, which was lavish, and always had been if an old turn-of-the-century photograph of their *Batavia* is any guide.

Above: Family group aboard a Potter's boat at Wheelock, c.1950.

Left: *Speedwell* approaching Wardle Junction, Middlewich. Date unknown but perhaps mid-1940s.

The *Euston* was built in 1912 by Samuel Fox at Longport near Tunstall on the Trent & Mersey for John Walley's small fleet and was docked by Tommy Williams at Kings Lock, Middlewich. Once again the boat carries the elaborate decoration of Bill Hodgson who was the painter there before he moved to the Anderton Company. The Whalley Canal carrying business had been established in the mid-nineteenth century, specialising in the purchase, carriage and sale of flints to the pottery industry, with some return traffic in crated ware. Flint calcinated to powder was an important ingredient of pottery 'slip', contributing to its translucency. Flints came up from Essex where a business was set up at Thurrock and from Normandy where an agent was employed. The Essex flints were brought up to Brentford for transfer to canal boats whilst the Norman ones went to Weston Point whence the Walley fleet took them up to the Potteries. The canal boats never numbered more than six, all horse drawn until motor boats were introduced after the Second World War by John's daughter Nora Walley to try and improve business. One was the *Dunstan* which they bought from John Knill (see page 83) but in the end road transport triumphed and canal activities ceased in 1953. The Thurrock business, however, continued as a supplier of calcinated flints for civil engineering works including the making of motorway verges.

Walley's last motor boat *Dunstan* working uphill at Wheelock in 1952

Salt Union

By the late-nineteenth century British salt production had become ruinously competitive. In an effort to rationalise and at the same time monopolise, London financiers established The Salt Union as an organisation to amalgamate the activities of the Cheshire, Staffordshire, Worcestershire and Teesside salt producers. Established in 1888 it not only took over the steam packets and dumb barges on the Weaver operated by the Cheshire firms, but also craft on the Tees and fleets of narrow boats in Worcestershire and Cheshire. The *Sabrina* was built in 1890 for John Corbett of Stoke Prior, probably at George Farrin's dock near Stoke but it passed to the Salt Union in 1895. *Sabrina* was the mythological nymph of the River Severn and the boat is illustrated in Hugh Conway-Jones' history of Gloucester Docks published in 1984, while the *Ireland* is portrayed in Peter Lead's pictorial survey of the Trent & Mersey published in 1980. Both pictures are in black and white and colour interpretation has been by scrutiny of the tones backed by information on the Salt Union colours in the North West from two Cheshire boatmen, Tommy Appleton and Harry Theobalds. The Cheshire boats worked along the Bridgewater and over the Rochdale canals, and some were built shorter to be able to carry on down the Calder & Hebble navigation and Sir John Ramsden's canal to Huddersfield. The *Ireland*'s registration number is a guesstimate, I'm afraid.

Salt Union's *Sabrina* with bye-trader's boats in the basin at Gloucester Docks, c.1895.

Henry Seddon & Sons were based in Middlewich but had associate companies in London and Dublin, with coasting steamers as well as canal craft. The first of their two Middlewich salt works were acquired in the late 1890s, the second in 1911 and as both were canalside they built up a fleet of narrow boats to bring in coal and send away salt. Most of it went to Anderton where it was transhipped to flats and steam packets on the Weaver for the run down to Liverpool and Birkenhead Docks for export. Seddons' last steam packet was the *Weaver Belle* built in 1900, paired with the large Mersey dumb flat *Gowanburn*. Boatbuilders for Seddon's were W. E. Costin of Berkhamsted and Nurser's of Braunston where the *Badger* was built in 1923. Animal names became most usual after a mixed selection which included *Nora* and *Jean*, Henry Seddon's grand-daughters. Boats were horse-hauled and trips were usually short, Middlewich to Anderton and back. No motor appeared until 1948 when the *Sweden* arrived from the Anderton Company but others followed and it became the usual practice for one motor to haul two butties to Anderton on this lock-free length. Their horses usually pulled two boats as well. The docking was undertaken by Tommy Williams at Kings Lock and then, when he closed, at the Anderton Company dock at Middleport, so Seddon's boats all carried the 'knobstick' style painting of Bill Hodgson. The narrow boats and river barges were all given up in 1960.

The Shropshire Union Railway and Canal Company, formed in 1846 by an amalgamation of several older canals with the recently constructed Birmingham and Liverpool Junction, very quickly developed a carrying fleet to operate over their own network, and into Birmingham and the Potteries. At the end of the nineteenth century they were running river tugs, barges, canal flats and about 300 narrow boats, mostly built at their own dock in Chester. Some

Seddon's boats at Sun Mills, Salford Docks in the 1940s.

of them were built specifically for their extensive fly boat service which delivered high value goods and parcels to a scheduled timetable, and these were built lighter with fine lines to travel faster and more easily behind a relay of fresh horses. *Symbol* was one of these boats, built at the small S.U. dock at Trevor, close to the Pontcysyllte aqueduct. Her commercial career had ended in 1954 as a station boat on the B.C.N. where she had worked for much of her life, under the S.U.C.& R.Co., then from about 1924 the London Midland & Scottish Railway and from 1948 the London Midland Region of British Railways. (see page 16) Subsequently she was converted to pleasure use but finally measured and dismantled in 2001, back at Trevor where she was built.

Barlow's Coal

Much of London's factory coal came from pits near Coventry – Bedworth, Nuneaton, Tamworth and Polesworth, much of it carried via the Grand Junction, now the Grand Union Canal. Around 1870 a young Samuel Barlow of Bedworth started a coal business with a pair of horse boats which grew steadily until, at its peak in 1944, it was running a fleet of over 70 long distance boats plus a fleet of B.C.N.- style day boats. They also acted as an agent and coal factor for many more of the individually owned boats of the 'Number Ones' and several of these boats and crews came into the Barlow's fleet during the 1930s and 40s when the new Grand Union Co. started competing for this traffic. (see page 95) But Barlow's post-war decline was rapid as road competition grew, and in 1962 they gave up their canal operations and continued with motor vehicles. The wooden butty *Rosie Agnes* shown here was acquired in 1935 from Joseph Rice, a Stroud carrier. She had been built in 1913, possibly by Walkers of Rickmansworth as the *Leighton* for Emanuel Smith, going to Rice in 1930 with the motor *Speedwell*.

From about 1914 they had their own dock at Glascote near Tamworth but much of their work was put out to the Nurser Brothers' yard at Braunston, whose business Barlow's finally bought in 1941. Frank Nurser, a very well-respected boat painter as well as a boatbuilder, stayed on as the manager and together with George Crowshaw from Glascote, they maintained the company's very high standard of decoration until the end. The dark green cabin sides and boldly shaded lettering were distinctive and the use of roses and castles on the outside was encouraged by the company for they saw no economic disadvantage in attention to decoration. Indeed the publicity which the company gathered outweighed the cost – witness the magnificence of the *Cairo* and *Warwick* at the 1950 Market Harborough Festival and Rally.

Not surprisingly there has been confusion between Samuel Barlow and S. E. Barlow, different fleets run by the same family. Samuel Edwin (S.E.) Barlow was a grandson of the original Samuel Barlow and started a separate carrying and coal merchant's business in 1919 at the Anchor Works, Glascote, near Tamworth, following this up with the Anchor Dockyard nearby. His fleet was never as large as the other but they had a similar colour scheme. The first motor boat came in 1935 and the one illustrated, the *Caen*, was bought in 1945. She had been the *Elizabeth* of the Erewash Canal Carrying Co., built in 1926 as a horse boat for Edward Lane. She was motorised in 1931/2 and sold to the Erewash in 1942. Eventually in 1957 the S. E. Barlow boats were taken over by the Samuel Barlow Company, but the *Caen* had already been disposed of.

Rosie Agnes at Braunston in the mid-1940s, just outside Nurser Brothers' dock where she was painted.

A. Wander Ltd., the Swiss firm, opened their Ovaltine factory alongside both canal and railway at King's Langley, north of Watford, in 1913. At first coal was brought by other carriers, but in 1925 they ordered the first of their own motor boats and butties from Walker's of Rickmansworth, the *Albert* and *Georgette*. Wander family names and others followed. Seven pairs were built before the war, but the company needed more and during the 1940s, three more pairs and a single motor were bought from the Grand Union fleet, all wooden and all built at Walkers. The *Enid* shown here left Rickmansworth in 1935 as the *Ursa* and came to Wanders in 1941 remaining in service until 1959, the last year of Ovaltine boat operation. They transferred something of their advertising house

Ovaltine butty awaiting docking at Bushel Bros' Dock at Tring about 1935.

style to their boats, including both the trademark lamp like Aladdin's and their slogan 'Drink Delicious Ovaltine', which appeared on both cratch and cabin side but there was much traditional decoration too. Their boats were maintained to the highest standards at Nurser's yard at Braunston.

Another company specialising in the carriage of coal was that of John Griffiths of Bedworth who had a big trade off the Coventry and Ashby canals. The Griffiths organisation was remodelled in the early 1930s as the Warwickshire Canal Carrying Co., the black cabin sides inherited from John Griffiths giving the fleet the name of 'Black Warwicks'. The *Alice* was built in 1907, probably by Nursers, for the Wolvercote Mill Co. of Oxford. She was bought by John Griffiths in 1919 and motorised in 1936. In 1941 she was sold to the Grand Union who leased her to their Erewash subsidiary. (see page 73)

Beautiful paintwork and snow white scrubbed ropework on *Enid*'s rams head, mid- 1950s.

Fore-ends & Cabin Details

Here are some other details of narrow boats – cratches, fore-ends, cabin backs, slides and hatches from Ovaltine and Barlow boats. The former used their cratches as they used their cabin sides, for advertising, while Barlows displayed more Nurser boatyard-style roses. The Ovaltine motor boat *Albert*, built by W.H. Walker & Bros Ltd. in 1925, was with the butty *Georgette*, the first of their fleet and is now restored and on display at Rickmansworth. The Barlow details come from several motor boats, the *Gort*, the *Malta* and the *Hardy*, an attractive feature of the last being the inside of the engine hole doors with their Y symbols.

Opposite page left: Motor boat *Hardy* with decoration by George Crowshaw at Braunston, July 1961.

Opposite page right: Ovaltine pair *William* and *Enid* awaiting unloading at the Kings Langley works, April 1956.

The 'Knobstick' painter Bill Hodgson worked latterly for the Anderton Company at their Middleport dock where, they docked boats for John Green, the Macclesfield carrier. Green concentrated on coal to the mills on the Macclesfield and Peak Forest canals, his boats not having side or top cloths, while his motors were distinctive, because they had square window-like portholes. The *Duchess of York* was not a locally built boat; she came from Nursers in 1933 so must have originally been painted in the Braunston style, but she is shown here as decorated by Mr Hodgson, with his readily recognised naturalistic style of roses and centrally placed many-turreted castles, often complete with swans in the foreground. In 1955 John Green gave up carrying. He had already sold two pairs in 1954, including the *Duchess of York*, to the newly formed Wyvern Shipping Co. (see page 73) and in 1955 his last pair, the *Sheila* and her butty *Prince of Wales*, went to Mersey-Weavers.

Jonathon Horsefield of Runcorn had deep, six plank narrow boats which would carry 30 tons of coal from the South Lancashire pits to merchants and gasworks along the line of the Bridgewater Canal;

indeed they were too big to leave it for the narrow system. The boats were mostly built by Simpson Davies at Runcorn to a distinctive design, full bodied with a straight stem and projecting timber-heads, and a low cabin as the boats were so deep. The hold was stiffened by fixed iron cross beams but stands, top planks, cratch and cloths were not usual as the cargoes did not need protection. Their motor boats, of which the *Richard* was one, were converted from horse boats, a counter being built round the original stern that retained the original style of horse boat helm. Similar in appearance and colours were the boats of J.E. Southern of Manchester and Simpson Davies themselves who ran the building dock at Runcorn. Naming of the boats was shared between the three fleets, all first names like *Agnes* and *Elizabeth*. The *Richard* was paired with *Winifred* when the Runcorn Gasworks traffic finished in 1962.

Above: Harry and Sarah Bentley with their Jon. Horsefield boats *Richard* and *Winifred* at Barton about 1955.

Left: Horsefield pair *Loretto* and *Marjorie* entering Barton swing aqueduct, August 1956.

Sand and Cement

London's expansion maintained a demand for building materials and roadstone, much of which came by water from canalside quarries and gravel pits. The *Evelyn* belonged to George Garside, a Leighton Buzzard quarry owner. She was built of wood in 1906 for Ireland & Knight of Mancetter Quarries, Nuneaton, but after a few years she passed to W. Clarkson of Vauxhall, London, and then in 1920 to George Garside who converted her into a motor boat in 1936. As a horse boat she almost always worked with the horse boat *Linney* under the same series of owners, until the *Linney* too became a motor in the same year. Both remained in traffic until about 1946.

Allied to the sand and gravel traffic was the use of the canals by the cement industry to distribute their products. Charles Nelson & Co. Ltd. of Stockton near Southam in Warwickshire were cement manufacturers who in 1885 had three steamers built for their London traffic by William H. Green of Polesworth, the *Jason* illustrated here and the *Janus* and *Jupiter*. They were wooden hulled and had large diameter Cochrane vertical boilers which protruded above the cabin top and two-cylinder simple expansion engines with, one imagines, two cranks. The number 1389 on the stern cabin side is the company number at Waterman's Hall whilst 9268 on the engine room is the boat's registered number there. Her capacity is 12 tons 6 cwt, and 7633 is a gauging number, most probably for the Warwick & Napton Canal. All three steamers passed to the Leighton Buzzard carrier L.B. Faulkner in 1912 who converted them to motors, although Charles Nelson continued with boats until about 1943. There is no certainty that green was the Nelson colour but examination of the black and white photographs suggest green as likely.

Steamer *Janus* on Sephton's Dock at Polesworth in the 1890s.

Portland Cement

Portland is a generic name for building cement, much of which is made in Oxfordshire and Warwickshire, where the canals were used to send away the finished product. The Oxford Portland Cement Company had a works at Kirtlington, eleven miles north of Oxford and used a fleet of ten narrow boats named after nearby villages, one of which was the *Tackley*. She was built by Nursers of Braunston in 1911 and stayed with the cement company until 1930. Much of the traffic was short haul, from the works to a wharf by Bletchington station, two miles away on the main Great Western line between Oxford and Wolverhampton. Here a hand crane transhipped from boat to covered railway wagon. Covered is here the operative word for the boats had coamings and hatchboards similar to those in a ship, the latter made waterproof by covers held down by battens and wedges.

Kaye & Company had a works on their own arm of the Warwick & Napton Canal near Southam and ran a small fleet of narrow boats, some of their own, others under contract, carrying cement, mainly to Birmingham. Their *Blue Lias* was named after the local clay from which the limestone for the cement manufacture is extracted. She was built by Nursers in 1923 and remained with Kaye & Co. until 1935 when she was sold to S.E. Barlow of Tamworth and renamed *Nelson*. Kaye

& Co. became part of the Rugby Portland Cement Company in 1934. The colours of *Blue Lias* are conjectural as I only have a black and white picture. The inscription on the blue diamond seems probable, though not proven.

Blue Lias on the Stratford Canal about 1923, approaching the drawbridge at Shirley.

London Boats

Southwold was a wide boat, a type much used in the London area, on the lower Grand Junction below Berkhamsted and on the Regent's Canal. They had capacities of up to 40 tons, sometimes more, but their load was dependent on depth of water. Because of the wide locks they could get to Braunston but were not encouraged to as no-one could pass them in the tunnels. They were not full lock width, but 9-13ft at gunwale level rounded in to 7ft at the bottom, which enabled them to swim better in the confined cross section of the canal. They were simply wide narrow boats, built in the same way with, in some cases, the full set of stands, planks, cratch and cloths. Many however were for bulk cargoes – sand, gravel and rubbish which needed no protection. Sabeys of Paddington & Acton were suppliers of building materials to, as Alan Faulkner says, 'the insatiable London Market'. They ran wide boats up as far as the sand quarries at Leighton Buzzard and the gravel pits at Rickmansworth. Boats were first acquired from other

Below & right: Sabey wide boats *Southwold* and *Abbeville* unloading at Marylebone power station in the 1930s, although the cargo appears to be crushed limestone or gravel.

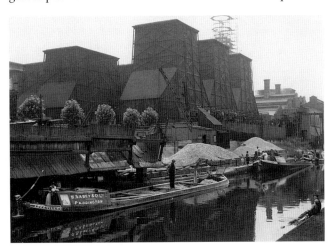

carriers but from the 1920s they were ordered new, the 13ft 3in beam *Southwold* being delivered in March 1930. She could carry 68 tons if the depth of water allowed. Sabeys had by this time a fleet of some thirty craft, including tugs. They remained in business up to the late 1940s.

Emanuel (sic) Smith had been in business since the 1880s based at Brentford with barges and narrow boats, the barges designed for both canal and river use. He had tugs and some motor narrow boats which he pioneered at the southern end of the Grand Junction, the first the *Premier* in 1912, and another the *Hasty* of 1919 built by Walkers at Rickmansworth. In 1923 the business was restyled E. Smith & Sons but its life was short for in late 1930 the fleet was sold off. The *Daventry* was built by Nursers of Braunston in 1907 but sold in 1930 to John Griffiths of Bedworth, the coal carrier. Note how the name is split by the anser pin, while the gauging numbers are prefixed by J (Grand Junction) and T (Thames).

Despite the look of the funnel, *Victoria* is not a steamer but one of the four large steel 'Royalty' class motors built by W.J.Yarwood of Northwich for Associated Canal Carriers, a small firm bought in 1930 by the new Grand Union Canal Carrying Company Limited. They were designed to work on the tidal Thames as well as the canal and were fitted with water ballast tanks, anchors and lifebuoys. *Victoria* herself was completed in October 1931 and was powered with a 22hp Kromhout engine, and was paired with the wooden butty *Albert* (of course), one of two built by Bushell Brothers of Tring. Both the motorship style funnel and the top part of the cabin chimney were hinged, the latter with a counterbalance, but neither feature remained for long, although the Grand Union persisted with funnels in their immense fleet and a few survived into nationalisation. The ornate and impressive decoration was short lived too giving way to the Grand Union's simpler practical style (see page 53) whilst the two shades of green were replaced by blue. *Victoria* became a maintenance boat in 1945 but was later acquired by the Birmingham & Midland Canal Carrying Co. and worked as the *Linda* for several years.

Looking back, the persistence of narrow boat carrying into the 1950s and 60s made poor economic sense, but at the time this did not seem so and many attempts were made, backed by the Inland Waterways Association, to keep these craft in business. There seemed to be openings for smaller operators if steady contracts could be secured, not involving large tonnages. The most ambitious enterprise and the best remembered was Willow Wren, started in 1953 by Leslie Morton, a former Cunard officer who had managed the Grand Union Canal Carrying Co. before the war. Perhaps it will suffice to say here that it was a brave effort dogged by misfortune. It needed much financial assistance, provided by the munificent Bulkeley-Johnsons whose boat *Willow Wren* gave the company its name, yet even when they withdrew in 1963 Leslie Morton carried on by leasing the boats to their captains. Sadly Morton died in 1968 and this finished the enterprise. They acquired boats from many sources, the *Swan* being an ex GUC Co. steel motor boat built by Harland & Wolff at North Woolwich, originally named the *Dunstable*. She went to Flixborough Shipping at Horninglow near Burton but in 1950 was bought by John Knill who changed the name to *Dunstan*.

He sold her to John Walley who resold her to Willow Wren in 1957 renaming her *Swan* to fit their bird naming policy, although the willow wren portrait on the cabin side was not over-accurate. However the boats were well-decorated.

Opposite page left: *Victoria* and *Albert* empty on the Wendover arm in the mid-1930s.

Opposite page right: Willow Wren's *Avocet* and butty passing Braunston in July 1961.

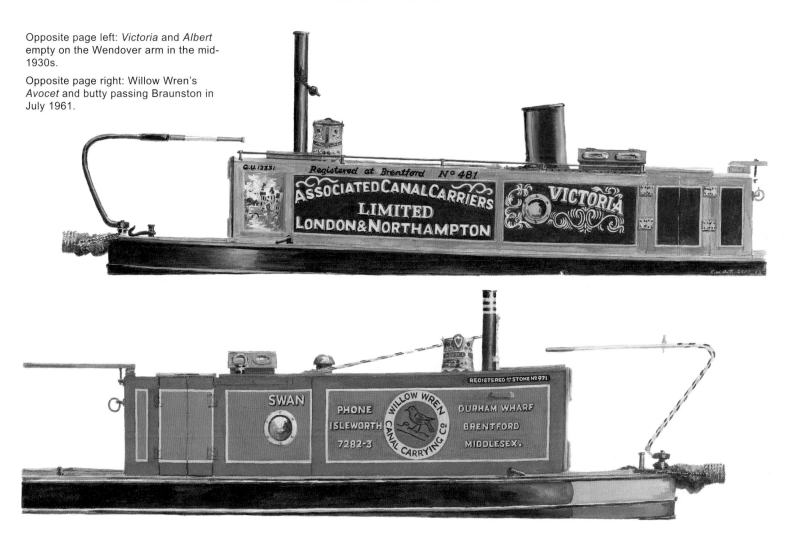

Of all the narrow boats that have survived, those of the Grand Union Canal Carrying Co. are the most numerous. The 1929 amalgamation of the canals from London to Birmingham and the Derby-Nottingham coalfield was a brave attempt to create a modern commercial system but it could only pay if the company won traffic for a carrying fleet which they would have to supply. Wide boats were proposed for the enlarged London to Birmingham line but they created passing problems, notably in the tunnels, so narrow boats had to be built. A boat building programme started in 1934, wood at first, then iron and steel composite, finally all steel. From the first modest orders when the company were feeling their way, the management became bolder and ended in 1938 with a fleet of 374 boats. All saw some service, but older ones were laid up, sold, or used for maintenance as newer ones arrived. About 120 pairs were the maximum in service at any one time. Crewing was the problem; with hindsight the enterprise looks over-ambitious, but the G. U. did prove its worth during the Second War and the boats

carried on to form a major component of the British Waterways nationalised carrying fleet. There are still a few in traffic and examples remain of all the various types ordered by the G.U.C.C.Co.

There were two main classes, the 'Stars' delivered between 1934-36 and the 'Towns' delivered between 1936-38. The 'Star' class boats illustrated here came from various builders. The *Merope* of 1936 is a wooden motor from Walker's of Rickmansworth (a 'small Ricky') while the *Nebulae* of 1935 was a steel butty from Harland and Wolff at North Woolwich (a 'small Woolwich'). *Regulus* was built by W.J.Yarwood at Northwich in 1935, one of the small number of 4ft 6in depth of hold 'Middle Northwich' size with rounded bilges and vee bottoms. The earlier (*Merope*) livery was changed to red, white and blue in 1937 to mark the Coronation of King George VI. The address and telephone number was altered several times and the fleet number was moved around on the butties. The overall effect was overcrowded and utilitarian, not owing much to canal tradition, but the company was determined to advertise its business.

There were no exterior flowers or castles, not even a symbol on the cabin slide, but the boat crews would continue to decorate the interior in the old way and use flower painted cans, although the company provided these in plain colours.

Note that the *Regulus* carries the early style of fleet number 79b
introduced in March/April 1936 but replaced in early 1937 by 343.
Initially the butties had no fleet numbers, only the motors.

The 'Town' class *Fulbourne* is a steel 'Large Woolwich' built by Harland & Wolff at North Woolwich in 1937, with a hold depth of 4ft 9½ins. British Waterways sold her in 1963 into private ownership for pleasure cruising, while she was also involved in a community project and spent some time as a houseboat. Now she is once more restored her to her original working appearance.

Austerity and utility were two hard-worked words during the Second World War – 'Austerity' locomotives built for the War Department, 'Utility' clothes and furniture for the people. Both meant cutting down to essentials and in the fleet of the Grand Union Canal Carrying Co., this was achieved in part by simplifying the company's title, so saving time and labour on the dock. The pre-war cabin side, crowded with full company name, address and telephone number was abandoned in favour of initials, fleet number

and boat's name. The decoration was slightly simplified too with a white dividing line along the top only. Once applied in the early 1940s this austere decoration remained until nationalisation in 1948 and could still be seen into the 1950s on boats not yet docked under the new regime. The *Aldgate* was a 'Town' class motor boat built by Harland & Wolff at North Woolwich in 1936, an all steel 'Large Woolwich'.

Above: Sampson Road Wharf in 1938, the main Grand Union depot in Birmingham.

Left: The Grand Union fitter's van on call to *Merope* in the late 1930s

Of all the British carrying fleets that of Fellows, Morton & Clayton Ltd., must be the best known. It was the largest in numbers of boats and range of operations and offered comprehensive warehousing plus, from the 1920s, its own road delivery service. The secret was in choice of cargo, never bulk, always cased and bagged goods, sugar, tea, soap, sauces, vinegar and metals, all commanding high freight charges. The boats were run economically with considerable management skill. The company always showed a profit except during the 1914-18 war and during their last year 1948, and it was the loss made then which made them decide to sell up to the Docks & Inland Waterways Executive.

The origins of the company date back to the boats of James Fellows who set up business in 1837. His company prospered and by 1860 was being run by James' son Joshua, whence came the company nickname of 'Joshers'. Frederick Morton was in partnership by then and by the 1870s they were big enough to buy the Bridgewater's narrow boats and those of the Grand Junction

Skipper Alf Walley with motor boat *Eagle* on the Shropshire Union in the 1930s.

too when they gave up carrying, including three of the first steam driven narrow boats. Steam hardly makes economic sense in these small capacity craft because the space needed for the engine, boiler and fuel reduce the cargo capacity to only 10 to 14 tons. But they were tireless and reliable and to make these steamers pay they were worked fly or non-stop from City Road and Brentford in London to Birmingham, Leicester, Nottingham and Derby, towing butties wherever possible. Effectively they were carrying tugs in continuous use, loading and discharging quickly. The final amalgamation was with the old established firm of Thomas Clayton in 1889 which brought them more boats and a dock at Saltley in Birmingham.

Their steamer *Empress* shown here was originally built of steel at the Fazely Street, Birmingham dock in 1887 but she was rebuilt in 1898 at the Saltley dock with iron sides. F.M.& C. eventually had 26 steamers in traffic before they were phased out in favour of motor boats. Their decoration was dignified, the original Fellows-Morton black and white with a red bead and a red cant, with slight variations of lettering style, spacing and scrollwork. Castles on the outside of the cabin were not a Fellows Morton adornment. In 1919 *Empress* was refitted as the motor boat *Envoy,* retaining her noticeably swept up counter, a steamer feature.

By the later 1900s the oil engine had become compact and reliable for use in small craft. Particularly good was the Swedish Bolinder, a semi-diesel hot bulb engine which was pioneered on the canals by Cadbury Brothers and the Grand Canal Company in Ireland but adopted with alacrity by Fellows, Morton & Clayton in 1912, who kept them to the end in 1948. Twenty-two steamers were converted, the last in 1927 and by 1939 there were 128 motor boats in service. Horse powers varied, 15, 10, 9, the last designed to run singly, with a generous cargo capacity of over 25 tons. These were the 'Fish' class, 18 in all, two wooden, twelve iron composite and four steel. The *Rudd* of 1936 is one of this group, built by Yarwoods but

fitted out by F.M.& C. at Saltley, and she carries the later colour scheme introduced in the 1920s. The old black and white colours were replaced by red with a green surround parted by a yellow bead. (see also pages 2 and 3) The large heavily shaded letters were bordered by simpler scrolls and bold horizontal lines broken by roundels.

The steamers working the wide locks of the Grand Junction route from London to Birmingham pioneered the idea of a powered boat pulling a dumb boat behind it, the motor and butty system that steadily superceded the old horse boats as the twentieth century progressed. The wooden *Buckby* was built in 1889 at the Fellows-Morton dock at Uxbridge and was photographed as a steamer butty around 1900, and remained a 'josher' until 1915 when it was sold to Cadbury Brothers Ltd. as a milk collecting boat. F.M.& C. had something like two hundred butties at the peak of their operations, either all wood or iron composite, that is with iron side and elm bottom boards. Much of the building was undertaken by Fellows-Morton themselves at Saltley and Uxbridge, the former turning out composite hulls, the latter wooden. Other builders for the company were Braithwaite & Kirk of West Bromwich, Harris of Netherton, whilst for wooden craft Costins of Berkhamsted, Lees & Atkins of Polesworth and Sephton's at Hawksbury. Twenty-five butties were bought from the Shropshire Union when they gave up carrying and up to a dozen from Midlands & Coast. The last wooden butty to be built for Fellows-Morton was the *Joan* which was completed at Uxbridge in 1933 and which survived into British Waterways days. (see page 3) Butties, with their generous display of gauging numbers on the cabin sides, followed motors into the red and green colour scheme from the mid 1920s, although steamers kept the black and white to the end.

Above: Fellows-Morton butty *Ipswich* working up Wolverhampton Locks, late 1940s.

Left: A Josher pair near Knowle on the Grand Union in 1955, still in F.M.& C. colours although by then operated by British Waterways.

Of the general carriers in the Leighton Buzzard area, two have remained well-known – L. B. Faulkner of Leighton Buzzard and A. Harvey Taylor of Aylesbury. Faulkner entered canal carrying as early as 1899 and expanded his fleet in the decade before the First World War. Boats were built and second hand ones acquired including three steamers from Charles Nelson. (see page 45) Silica sand from local pits for glass making was the main business. Faulkner acquired the dock at Linslade in the 1920s and it continued in business after his death in 1950, eventually closing in 1956. The last foreman there was the renowned boat painter Frank Jones. The carrying fleet declined rapidly after the Second War and the last boats were sold in 1951. Most of the boats were named after birds. *Vulture* was built in 1904 by W. E. Costin of Berkhamsted, motorised in 1933 and sold in 1950 as a holiday cruise boat with the name *Wanderer*.

Arthur Harvey-Taylor of Aylesbury acquired the boats of another Aylesbury carrier John Landon in 1923 and expanded, introducing

motor boats in 1924. Like Faulkners, Harvey-Taylor won traffic from local quarries, but coal was a staple with timber cargoes to Aylesbury and, during the Second War, a bit of variety including sand, strawboard and aluminium billets to be cast into aircraft engine cylinders in Birmingham. However by the 1950s the fleet was much reduced and in 1955 the last two pairs were sold to Samuel Barlow. The wooden *Daphne* was one of the butties sold, paired with the *Roger*. The *Daphne*, formerly the *Rose of Sharon*, had been built in 1930 for the Grand Junction Number One, Joseph Grantham, but was bought by Harvey-Taylor in 1937. Barlows sold her on in 1961. Harvey-Taylor colours and decoration were not extravagant and the single digit telephone number will cause some amusement today. His boats were named after members of the family.

Above: *Roger* and *Daphne*, 1950s.

Left: A Faulkner boat iced in on the Northern Oxford Canal in the 1920s.

Narrow boating on the River Severn was dangerous because of the wild variations in level which created strong currents and floods. The experts were the boatmen of Gloucester, and Gloucester became the headquarters of the biggest river carrying business, Severn & Canal. This had early nineteenth century origins, late eighteenth even, in the Danks family of trow and boat owners. For most of the nineteenth century the Danks continued in business but in 1873 they merged with a competitor, the Severn carrying business of J. Fellows & Co, the Fellows of Fellows, Morton & Clayton, to form a new concern, later called the Severn & Canal Carrying Company. Trows, narrow boats and steam tugs made up the company's fleet and they had a steam coaster too, the *Atalanta*. (see page 157) In

spite of the profitability of the tugs the new company encountered financial problems. It was rescued by the Sharpness, New Docks & Gloucester & Birmingham Navigation Co. who took over the tugs in 1906 and the whole fleet in 1909. After the First World War the company was again in difficulties but was saved this time by one of their main customers, Cadbury's, the real saviour being that champion of inland waterways George Cadbury (1878-1954) who joined the Severn & Canal board in 1923 and later became chairman. With fresh capital and vigorous advertising much was done to build up the business.

As part of that advertising campaign the boats carried details of the company's services. *Motor No.8* illustrated here was originally the horse boat *Aldersley* built by Severn & Canal at their Stourport dock in 1913. She was converted to a motor in 1939 with a 15hp Bolinder and in 1948 was sold to Thomas Clayton of Oldbury, becoming their *Dove*. *M.V.4* whose stem is shown. Here was one of the motor boats acquired by Severn & Canal from Cadbury's when in 1928 the latter gave up their fleet. The butty *Wulfruna* was built in 1913 by J. E. Perry & Sons of Wolverhampton. She was named after the Lady Wulfrun who founded Wolverhampton's first church in 994 AD, and was sold in 1923, probably to Leonard Leigh.

Severn & Canal C. Co. boats waiting to unload at Cadbury's Bournville factory in the 1930s.

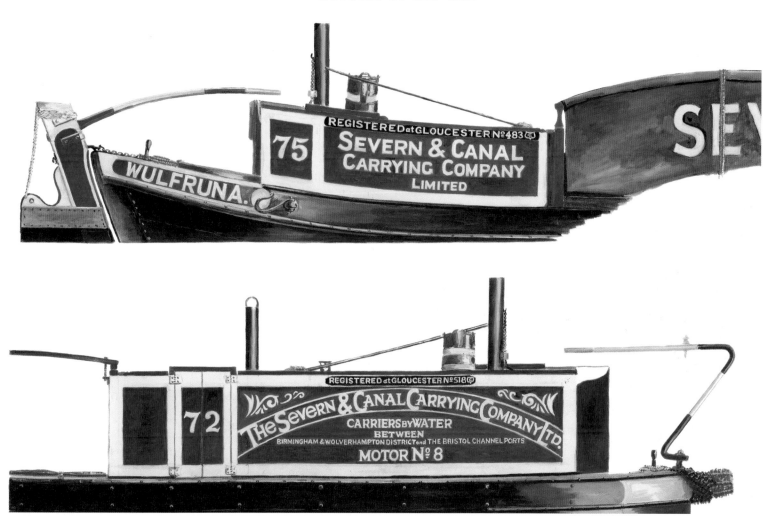

Some manufacturing firms of international stature ran fleets of narrow boats themselves. Cadbury's had a high regard for canal transport which indeed influenced their decision to move to Bournville alongside the Worcester & Birmingham Canal in 1879. When they later established other milk factories they chose canalside sites, in 1911 at Knighton near Market Drayton on the Shropshire Union, in 1915 at Frampton-on-Severn on the Gloucester & Sharpness and in 1922 a process factory at Blackpole on the Worcester & Birmingham. At Knighton local Cadbury horse boats collected milk in churns from canalside farms, while between the factories there was two way traffic, mass, pure ground cocoa from Bournville which was an ingredient of crumb, the dry mixture of cocoa, sugar and evaporated milk which was refined into chocolate. With much capital at their command Cadbury decided, after using other carriers and their own horse boats, to employ motor boats. Two were ordered of an unusual design from a works in Motherwell. They had a hull form quite unlike the traditional shape, a hold with

hatches, wheel steering and Bolinder engines. Delivered in 1911 they were among the pioneers but did not prove robust enough for canal work so were withdrawn. Eventually in 1915 the company turned to Walker's of Rickmansworth for motors and butties of conventional design. Their colours and lettering followed the Cadbury's house style, the one illustrated opposite giving way to a lower case lettering layout that was applied to their advertisements, chocolate wrappers and railway wagons. Boats continued to be built up to 1926 but from 1928 Cadbury's gave up boats and used other carriers, most notably the Severn & Canal Carrying Co. with which George Cadbury was closely involved. (see page 62)

Under the Cadbury influence Severn & Canal ordered eight new welded wrought iron motor narrow boats from the Bristol shipbuilders Charles Hill. At 72 feet these new 'Severners' were among the longest narrow boats in the country, and big, with a 30 ton capacity. In August 1934 the first two were delivered, the *Ash* and the *Oak*, which is now preserved at Gloucester Waterway Museum. Unusually their 10hp Petter engines were abaft the living cabin which was not popular with the boatmen. Moreover they were not powerful enough to handle a butty on the Severn, indeed they were underpowered for the river even by themselves. On nationalisation most went over to maintenance work, but two passed to the independent Gloucester carrier Charles Ballinger. (see page 75)

Opposite page left: Cadbury's Knighton factory on the Shropshire Union in the 1920s, with a local collection 'milk' boat tied in front of their motor *Bournville No 2*.

Opposite page right: Severner *Oak* in Birmingham, perhaps posing for a photograph whilst it was still quite new in 1934.

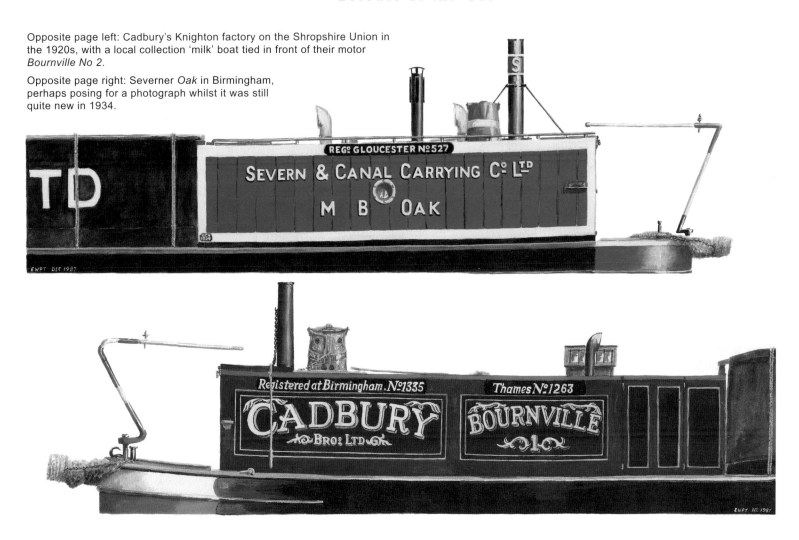

Nationalisation of transport on 1 January 1948 brought several carrying fleets owned by navigation authorities into the fold of a new body, the Docks & Inland Waterways Executive of the British Transport Commission. For convenience the inland waterways side of the Executive was christened British Waterways. The boats were a mixed crowd from the short boat fleet of Canal Transport on the Leeds & Liverpool to the keels of the Trent. Most of the narrow boats came from the enormous fleet of the Grand Union Carrying Co., with some following on in October from the Severn & Canal Carrying Co. (by then called Severn Carrying). These were joined in 1949 by the Fellows, Morton & Clayton fleet. A new colour scheme was needed to bind all these craft together, to give what later came to be called a corporate identity. At the suggestion of Robert Davidson, formerly general manager of the Leeds & Liverpool and now a member of the Executive, a startling livery of yellow and blue was chosen, with the yellow predominant. It found little or no favour for the colours were alien to canal tradition although freshly painted boats looked smart enough. Indeed there was quite a public outcry over the abandonment of traditional decoration and in 1949 the colour

Motor and butty *Stratford* and *Bideford* looking very newly painted in the 1950s.

British Waterways pair at Boxmoor in June 1956, the skipper picking up the towrope to his butty *Norton*.

predominance was reversed to blue and yellow, more balanced and effective, with early examples given extra embellishment by the various dock painters.

The *Henry* was a Grand Union steel 'Royalty' class motor boat built by James Pollock of Faversham in Kent in 1931, one of the big boats designed for river work as well as canal. It is doubtful if the *Henry* saw much commercial service but she has been chosen because the National Waterways Museum at Gloucester has an early yellow predominating over blue painting specification with the name of this craft on it. In fact by 1948 the *Henry* was on maintenance work only. Somewhat less dramatic craft followed the 'Royalties' in the G.U. fleet, first from 1934 the 'Star' class then from 1936 the steel 'Towns', deeper in the hold for cased goods. The earliest to be painted in the reversed colour scheme, with blue predominant, was the *Lancing* built by Yarwoods. Note the lining and fleur-de-lys added by the dock painter although these modest corner embellishments of 1949 did not long survive.

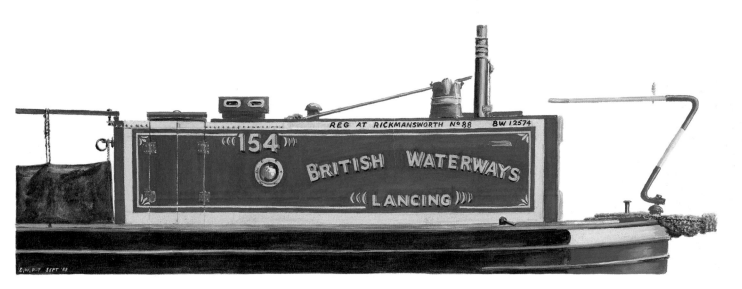

These two boats show each end of the evolution of British Waterways' livery styles. On nationalisation in 1948 the contentious yellow and blue appeared and the motor *Darley* and butty *Ayr* were so painted and much photographed to show off the new colours. The steel *Darley*, a 'Large Woolwich' built in 1937, has survived and after service as a dredger with Alfred Matty of Coseley was restored along with the butty *Alperton* to that original colour scheme in the 1980s.

The *Zodiac*, fleet number b10, is a refuelling craft on the Gloucester & Sharpness, serving the floating plant. She is believed to be the *Tucana* of 1936, one of the eight 'Middle Northwich' steel motors but she has acquired the name *Zodiac* although there is already another *Zodiac*, likewise a 'Middle Northwich'. Our *Zodiac* carries the green B.W. livery of the 1990s and the new leisure orientated logo which does not show to advantage on a boat although admirable perhaps as a letter heading. Since then yet another reorganisation within B.W. has introduced yet another change of corporate image and the green too has passed into history.

Above: Empty pair of B.W. boats heading south at Uxbridge in March 1956.

Left: Ex-Josher *Chiltern* working down Audlem Locks on the Shropshire Union, July 1959.

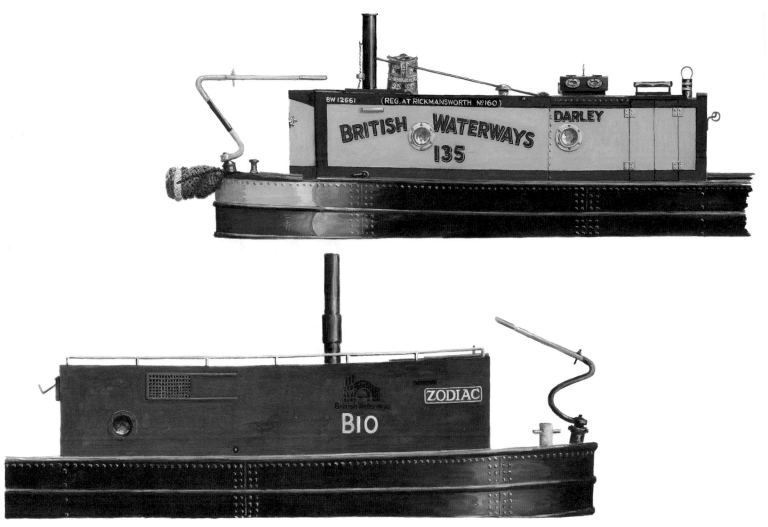

British Waterways III

The commercial narrow boat fleet that was run by British Waterways eventually settled for an azure blue and yellow livery. It was some time before the design settled down; earlier versions of the painting scheme were subject to the fancy of the dock painter, but the *Pegasus*, an iron composite Small Woolwich built by Harland & Wolff in 1935 with a 4ft 2in depth of hold, illustrates what became more or less standard. When freshly painted it was a smart livery, but blue does fade badly. The boat was acquired from B.W. in 1988 and a series of careful owners restored her to working trim. The only divergence from strict accuracy was the painting of real roses and castles on the cabin doors, instead of using the insipid transfers which B.W. had introduced, but who can complain about that?

The *Radiant*, a steel Middle Northwich motor boat of 4ft 6in depth of hold, was built in 1935 by W.J.Yarwood. Most of the *Radiant's* career has been on maintenance work on the Gloucester & Sharpness Canal with the fleet number B3. Before nationalisation and during the Second World War she was probably a pump boat for the fire service with a 3in bore centrifugal pump in the extension forward of the engine hole, driven off the Ruston & Hornsby engine, replaced in 1971 by a Lister. She is shown here in the simple maintenance boat colours of the 1970s-80s.

May 1956 at Nash Mills, with the earlier paintwork on *Cassiopeia* fading fast whilst the butty *Dodona* already carries the simpler plain blue livery.

The steel butty *Wye* has been restored and is preserved by the National Waterways Museum at Gloucester. She is one of the 'River' class 'blue tops', fitted with blue fibreglass hold covers instead of canvas top cloths, and was built in 1958 by the Thames Launch Works at Twickenham, along with five others in the first batch of these boats. They could carry 20% more cargo than conventional butties and were given extra long cabins to accommodate an Elsan toilet compartment. The *Wye* was in traffic until 1963 and thereafter on maintenance work on the Gloucester & Sharpness Canal until she came to the museum in 1993.

The Erewash Canal Company had started a subsidiary carrying business in 1927, a small canal with a small fleet, but busy with locally mined coal traffic. When the Grand Union acquired the canal in 1932 a new subsidiary was set up to develop that business, the Erewash Canal Carrying Co. It was expanded by the building of two steel pairs of narrow boats by Yarwoods of Northwich, delivered in 1935, the motor *Cyprus* and butty *Cedar*, and the motor *Ash* and butty *Elm*. *Cyprus* should surely have been *Cypress* but such misunderstandings seem to have been common among the dock painters especially when they had to unravel the 'Star' class naming of the Grand Union fleet. *Fomalhaut* started as *Formalhaut*, *Triangulum* appeared as *Triagulum* and *Galaxy* as *Glaxy*, all unfamiliar names unless you were an astronomer. Erewash cabin side layout followed the Grand Union pattern, informative but dull, using unattractive colours which would become nondescript after a few months service. The boats passed into nationalised hands along with the Grand Union fleet.

Members of the Grantham family on their Wyvern Shipping pair in 1958 or 1959.

Cyprus and *Cedar* photographed when new at Yarwood's shipyard on the river Weaver, 1935.

The Wyvern Shipping Co. was a relative latecomer, founded in 1954 by Lord Geoffrey Percy, brother of the Duke of Northumberland, and Michael Keef, with the backing of the Inland Waterways Association. They bought the motor *Heather Bell* from C. & D. March of Worcester (see page 83) and two pairs of boats from John Green, the Macclesfield carrier. For a short while they were able to keep in business but had to lay the fleet up in 1956 for lack of work. They survived because they went into pleasure cruising and flourish in this role today. The *Benevolence* was one of the motors from John Green and had been built by Nursers of Braunston for Green in 1938. She became first a six and then an eight berth cruiser and in 1961 a ten berth. She was sold in 1965. The Canada goose badge on the side designed by Peter Scott derives from Lord Geoffrey's own boat *Canada Goose* which he used for pleasure before Wyvern was founded. She too became a member of the Wyvern hire fleet.

The *Edna Grace* was one of the horse boats of the Gloucester carrier Charles Ballinger. She was built in 1912 but not acquired by him until 1929. At one stage of her career she was docked by Peter Keay & Son of Walsall as the date on the cabin side waterway shows. After Ballinger had her she went to S. Healing & Sons.

Quite different were the cabin colours of Charles Ballinger's motor boats of which he had three, two hired and then bought in 1950-52 from the former Severn & Canal fleet and one bought in 1953 from DIWE, ex Fellows, Morton & Clayton. The *Olive* was the *Beech* of Severn & Canal, one of the welded steel ones built by Charles Hill of Bristol in 1935 and sister to the *Oak*, displayed at Gloucester. Charles Ballinger carried chocolate crumb from Cadbury's milk factory at Frampton on Severn to Bournville and also worked for Samuel Morland & Sons Ltd., the Gloucester matchmakers. In 1962 Ballinger died and his fleet was given up.

Bridget carrying large coal for the Severn Dredger in July 1959, with the skipper preparing to strap the boat into a lock on the Tardebigge flight.

Corn Millers

Grain and flour were major traffics on many canals and it was common for mills to run their own boats. However the Shropshire Union hardly allowed anyone but themselves to carry on their canals, with a few exceptions like Griffiths of Chester. A. & A. Peate had a mill at Maesbury Hall near Oswestry on the Ellesmere Canal line to Llanymynech whilst Arthur Sumner had another at Wrenbury near Nantwich on the line to Hurlestone Junction. Both relied on the Shropshire Union's carrying fleet for grain and flour, so when the company ceased carrying in 1921, the two mills had no alternative but to quickly find boats of their own. This was relatively easy as the whole S.U. fleet was up for sale. Peates bought eight horseboats, one of them the famous *Cressy* named after a 1900s naval cruiser and eventually owned by L.T.C.Rolt. Others were named after First World War commanders and battles – *Sir John Jellicoe*, the *Lemburg* after the Russian victory over the Austrians in 1915, and this one the *Bethune* commemorating a sector of the Somme fighting. She was built in 1915-16 almost certainly at Chester. Under Peates the boats kept their Shropshire Union colours

with minor decorative alterations. The name of ownership was changed but the boat's name, usually carved in the top bend by the Shropshire Union, stayed. An exception seems to have been the *Bethune* whose name, according to a good photograph, appears to be painted. Peates went to John Beech's dock at Welsh Frankton and the old S.U. dock at Chester for repairs, leased in the 1920s to J. Harry Taylor, himself a good boat painter. He may have been responsible for the geometric design on the helm of the *Bethune*. She passed to the Mersey Weaver Co., in 1934, was sold to the

Above: Signwriting and decoration by J. Harry Taylor at his dock in Chester in the 1920s.

Left: One of the ex-Shropshire Union boats that formed the new Peate's fleet in the 1920s, seen outside the dry dock in Chester.

L.M.S.R. in 1945 and scrapped in 1949. Harry Taylor was responsible for the ornate work on Sumner's *Margaret*, another ex-Shropshire Union boat which the canalside mill at Wrenbury acquired after 1921. She was built in 1915 as the *Warfare*. The late J. Horace Taylor told me Sumners gave her a red cabin side and Harry Taylor added the elaborate Tuscan lettering which some carriers liked. The mill kept the *Margaret* until 1927. There is a good black and white photograph of her with details of the cabin but misses out the stern and helm, which is therefore supposition.

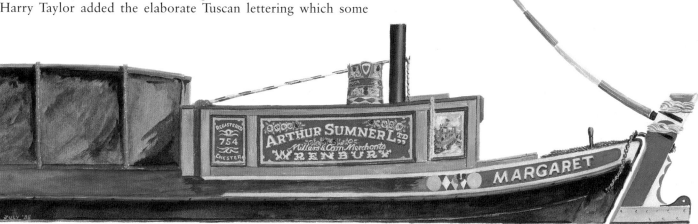

Proud Owners

Many people know of the Skinners, Rose and Joe, the last Number Ones on the Oxford Canal who kept going until 1959 with the *Friendship* pulled by their mule 'Dolly'. *Friendship* is now in the Boat Museum at Ellesmere Port, relatively safe for posterity because she is not afloat but indoors in a gallery. But he had a second boat, the *Elizabeth*, built in 1928 which he kept until 1944 when she was sold to Alfred Hone of Banbury, another Oxford Number One who renamed her *Duke of York*. Two years later she went over to Samuel Barlow who called her the *Oxford*, at the same time as they took over Hone's *Cylgate*. Like the *Friendship* the *Elizabeth* was probably built by Sephtons of Tusses Bridge near Hawksbury. Decoration is similar, both roses and castles probably painted by Tooleys of Banbury who certainly did the well-known work on *Friendship*.

The smaller fleets of narrow boats were often as decorative as the Number Ones for the same reasons, smart paintwork inspiring confidence. Moreover with not too many boats maintenance was easier and

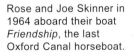

Rose and Joe Skinner in 1964 aboard their boat *Friendship*, the last Oxford Canal horseboat.

Wide boat *Golden Spray* resplendant with the paintwork of Bushell Brothers' Dock at Tring, seen here at Brentford in the 1930s.

particular attention could be given to decoration. The advertising aspect appealed to manufacturers who ran their own fleets like Ovaltine and Cadburys and to smaller firms like the canalside flour millers Tooveys of Kings Langley in Hertfordshire. Originally water powered, the mill went over to steam in 1894 and coal for the boilers came by canal as did the corn, from London Docks, transhipped into canal craft at Brentford. Flour left the mill the same way. Wide boats were mostly used and Tooveys had some of their own, the *Langley* built for them in 1916, and the *Betty* bought second hand. In 1922 *Betty* was replaced by the *Golden Spray* built, like the *Langley*, by Bushell Brothers at Tring. *Golden Spray* was the name under which the flour was sold and the boat was particularly resplendent with the most complex pattern of diamonds at both stem and stern, and elaborate Tuscan 'fish tailed' lettering on the cabin sides. She had a well-decorated fore cabin too. (see page 123) Tooveys gave up their boats in 1938 and the *Golden*

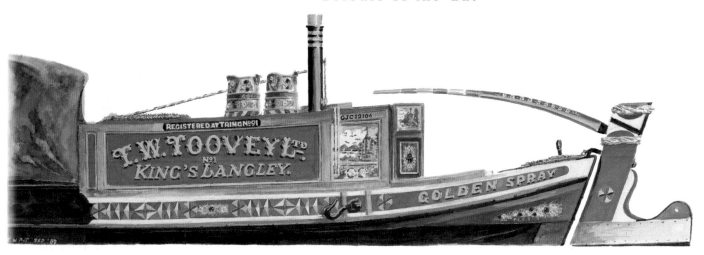

Spray passed to Thomas Clayton of Paddington who renamed her *Leonard* and put her into the rubbish traffic. Because of their greater width, wide boats had longer helms than conventional narrow boats.

Samuel Barlows gave up their boats and dock in 1962 but both were bought by Michael Streat who had been at Braunston for ten years with hotel boats and a hire fleet called Blue Line Cruisers. He continued carrying under the name of Blue Line Canal Carriers, initially with four pairs and a single motor, but he had reduced the fleet to three pairs when the contracts ran out and the last runs were made in October 1970. Among the last was the *Raymond* paired with the motor *Roger* and run by the Brays. The *Roger* came from the small Harvey-Taylor fleet bought by Barlow's in 1955, but the *Raymond* was built by Barlows at Braunston and launched on 2 June 1958, the last wooden butty to be completed by anyone anywhere for commercial carrying. Happily she was entirely rebuilt and restored in 2000 and her future now looks secure for many more years. The Blue Line ship's wheel symbol shown here was later dropped but the company continued to maintain the high standard of Barlow/Nurser paintwork and decoration to the end.

Gordon Waddington was a carrier based on the Bridgewater Canal, concentrating on coal but not to the exclusion of other cargoes. He started after the Second World War with a Leeds & Liverpool steamer and two wide boats in the coal trade from the Leigh pits to Runcorn gasworks. After a while he disposed of all these in favour of the ex-Ovaltine motor boat *Harry* which he renamed *Joyce*, and then *Rita*. More narrow boats were acquired in 1952 and an association began in that year with Lees & Atkins of Polesworth who docked and decorated the boats in their characteristic elaborate style. All craft were second hand, some ex-Fellows, Morton & Clayton, by then within British Waterways, and two from Cowburn & Cowpar, the *Swan* of 1933 and *Seagull* of 1935. (see page 97) The Waddington fleet was based at Leigh, handy for the collieries. Apart from Runcorn gasworks, coal went to Manchester, a day's trip which allowed a big tonnage to be carried. China clay to the potteries and spelter or zinc to Wolverhampton

were other cargoes with return loads of Trentham gravel to Trafford Park, but the end of the Runcorn gasworks traffic in 1962 forced Gordon Waddington to give up. It stopped Horsefields and

Above: Arthur Bray aboard his butty *Raymond,* tied up for Christmas at Braunston 1968.

Right: Gordon Waddington's pair *Galatea* and *Sirdar* on the Bridgewater Canal at Worsley, heading for Runcorn in August 1956.

Southerns too. His last acquisition had been a Grand Union pair, the 'Royalty' *William* and the butty *Princess.* Most of his fleet has survived in private hands for he kept going into the days of preservation, so securing a safe future for some interesting craft.

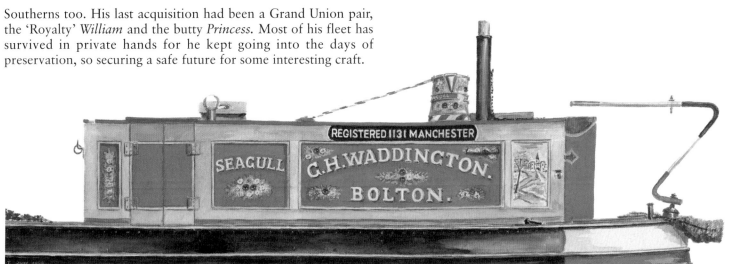

Well before the founding of the Inland Waterways Association in 1946 there were a few brave spirits who saw the canal system in a similar light and thought that commercial carrying especially by narrow boat should be maintained. They were adventurous enough to put their ideas into action. One pioneer was C. Payne Crofts of Northampton with his steam narrow boat *Sentinel* of 1927 powered by one cylinder of a Sentinel steam lorry engine. She did not prove a very successful craft, she was overpowered and there were problems of ash disposal. More rewarding were the efforts of Christopher March and his sister Daphne of Worcester who in 1937 ordered a motor narrow boat from Nursers of Braunston. They carried on holidays and at weekends until the Second War when

Heather Bell in the Black Country with Frank Nurser's paintings displayed, so perhaps soon after she was launched in 1937.

Christopher March went off to sea and Daphne started full time with their mother as crew in the *Heather Bell*. This was in 1941 and she was asked to train girls for work on the Grand Union. She refused because she did not want to leave home waters, the Worcester & Birmingham, the Gloucester & Sharpness and the B.C.N., and she sent her then mate Eily Gayford. After the war the Marches bought in 1946 a wooden Walker built butty the *Lambourne* from the Grand Union Canal Carrying Company but traffic was not the same and both were sold in 1954, the *Heather Bell* going to the new Wyvern Shipping Company. (see page 73) The Marchs had done a remarkable job which included work for Fellows, Morton & Clayton from Ellesmere Port to Wolverhampton, Birmingham and Nottingham.

John Knill was a post-war carrier. After naval service he bought the steel composite motor *Columba* in 1948, a 'small Woolwich' built in 1935, and the iron composite butty *Uranus*, another 1935 'small Woolwich' both built for the Grand Union fleet but by then owned by H. Dean & Sons of Manchester. More boats were added and work was found wherever possible. One wooden butty *Lucy* was built for him in 1955 by Samuel Barlow at Braunston. But at the end of the following year the fleet was sold off; most of the boats including the *Lucy* and the *Columba* went to Samuel Barlow. The long cabin on the *Columba* had been put in by the Deans. John Knill used it as an office when he worked the boat and the extension certainly improved living conditions. The full slogan on the cloths was 'USE INLAND WATERWAYS'. Boats were docked both at Braunston and by the Mersey Weaver at Middleport, Burslem, the latter painting the cabin panel surrounds dark royal blue rather than graining them.

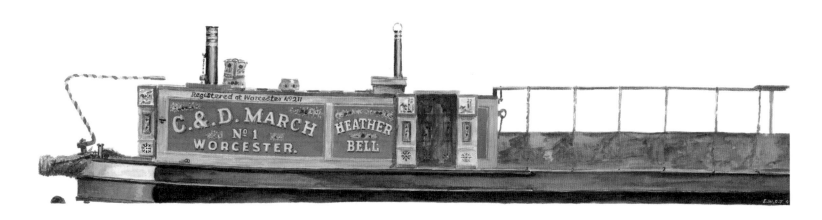

Here are a couple of recent East Midlands carriers who, like so many, were able to buy ex-Grand Union Canal Carrying Company boats and start a business. Kenneth Roseblade of Leicester partnered by his fiancée Jean Seymour started with local towage work on the Leicester Navigation and associated waterways and then undertook some long distance carrying when more boats had been acquired. Business had started in 1962 but although initially encouraging it did not stay that way and after about four years, carrying was given up although the company continued as waterways civil engineering contractors and established a marina and boatyard at Leicester. The *Neptune* was their first. She was among the three wooden prototype pairs built for the Grand Union Canal Carrying Company in 1934 by Walker's of Rickmansworth, the first of the 'star' class although in this case named after a planet. Samuel Barlow bought her in 1943 and she was sold to Seymour-Roseblade in 1961, the year

before Barlow's gave up their fleet. During their ownership Seymour-Roseblade made some minor colour and lettering alterations, including a bright red for the inside of the engine hole doors.

Threefellows were a more recent creation who concentrated latterly on gravel shipments from a quarry at Thurmaston on the Soar to a ready-mix plant at Syston a mile and a half downstream. This started in 1976, then ceased because of a ban on quarry extraction, but restarted in 1980 and continued until 1988. Four pairs were employed backwards and forwards, a traffic in which narrow boats could be competitive, a steady flow over a short distance. The *Buxton* was steel built for the Grand Union in 1937 by Harland & Wolff at North Woolwich, a 'large Woolwich'. British Waterways had her on various tasks until 1971 when she was bought by the Threefellows partnership. From 1973 to 1976 she worked

Above: Two pairs of the Threefellows' fleet at work on the gravel traffic on the River Soar in the early 1980s.

Left: Seymour-Roseblade boats *Jaguar* and *Crater* loaded with timber at Boston on the River Witham, August 1964.

on the Boxmoor limejuice contract, after which she transferred to the River Soar. Her colours are unusual for a canal boat and the lettering a departure from tradition, maybe intentionally so.

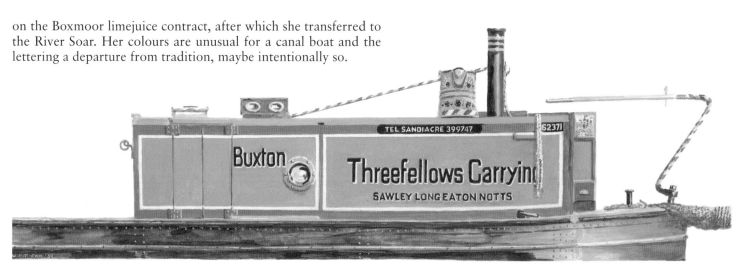

Knowledge of the colours of the carriers on the Kennet & Avon is slight but the maroon of the Midland Railway is a sensible guess, bearing in mind the livery of locomotives and coaches. The Midland narrow boat depicted will be recognised from the photographs of *No 3* at Dundas in K.R.Clew's history 'The Kennet & Avon Canal'. *No 3* was built in 1894 for the Midland who assembled a small fleet at Bradford-on-Avon to bring goods to the company's stations at Bath and Bristol. The venture did not last beyond the 1890s but had the merit of infiltrating Great Western territory. *No 3* passed to Robbins, Lane & Pinniger, the Honey Street, Pewsey, timber merchants, boat builders and canal carriers, in 1912.

The Great Western, as owners of the Kennet & Avon canal have been criticised for neglect and obstruction, but it was this very attitude which focussed attention on the canal and encouraged restoration, completed in 1990. Among the leaders of the Kennet & Avon crusade was John Gould of Newbury who acquired a small

fleet of boats from A. Harvey-Taylor of Aylesbury, starting with the motor *Colin* and butty *Iris* bought in 1949. His plan was to bring traffic to the Kennet & Avon to demonstrate that it had value. Cargoes came from Birmingham and went from Newbury down to Hampton on the Thames. Under the British Transport Commission, successors to the Great Western, a policy of discouragement was pursued and in May 1950 a stoppage was declared. Mr Gould had

Above: Boatbuilder and decorater Frank Jones of Leighton Buzzard at work on *Colin* in about 1950.

Left: Horseboat on the Kennet and Avon Canal near Bath, date unknown, but probably pre-Second World War.

to resort to local work but the navigation continued to deteriorate and eventually in 1955 he took the BTC to court and won compensation. By this time the *Colin* and *Iris* had become passenger trip boats. They had been built as the *Betty* and *Ann* in 1919 by Hilditch & Hilditch of Walsall for Nicholson & Son Ltd. of Maidenhead. Arthur Harvey-Taylor bought them in 1924 and renamed them *Colin* and *Iris* after his son and daughter. John Gould kept them together too and had them docked by L.B.Faulkner of Leighton Buzzard, where the painter was Frank Jones. The boats were disposed of in the 1960s.

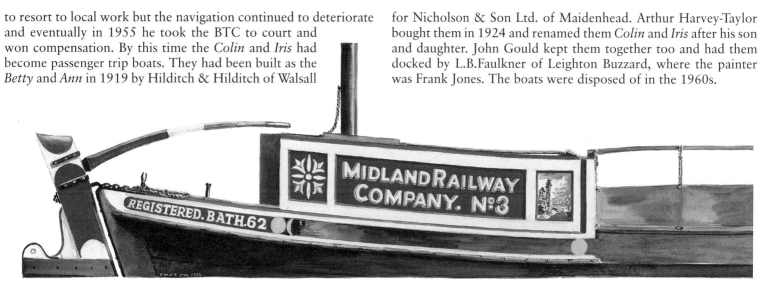

On narrow canals the carriage of liquids in bulk became the responsibility of several firms, most notably Thomas Clayton of Oldbury, who were descended from general carriers but in the later 19th century became liquid transport specialists, pursuing an independent career from 1889. They had used barrels and casks but in the 1880s decked over the holds to create miniature oil tankers. Holes were cut in the deck for loading and discharge but stability remained a problem. It was solved by building swillboards across the hold to check surge of the liquid, while motor boats were given bulkheads the full height of the hold with a paddle sluice so the cargo could be trimmed. Almost all Clayton boats were wooden, motors, butties and horse boats, these last having a good long foredeck under which the feed could be stored.

The *Doon* (all the boats were named after rivers) was built in 1919 by Nursers of Braunston. The motor boat *Spey* is a bit younger, built in 1937 by F.M.C. at Uxbridge for Thomas Clayton, along with other motors and butties in the later 1930s. She remained with Clayton's to the end, latterly as a spare boat but in earlier days she had been paired with the *Ohio*. Clayton's boats were always handsomely decorated, many at the Nurser Bros or Lees & Atkins boatyards, and at their own dockyard at Oldbury. Here boatbuilder/painter Fred Winnet continued the tradition until traffic ended in 1966.

Liquids could also be carried in tanks secured in the boat's hold. W. H. Cowburn & Cowpar of Manchester were chemical manufacturers with origins in the 1870s. From the 1900s they were running a fleet of flats and narrow boats carrying their products in casks, carboys and drums. The business grew in the 1920s because of the demands of Courtaulds, who were manufacturing artificial fibres at Coventy and Wolverhampton, so in 1932 they ordered two composite motor boats from Yarwoods for their general chemicals traffic. Following their evident success six more motor

Cowburn & Cowpar's *Seagull* at Yarwood's shipyard in Northwich, after refitting with the two bulk carbon disulphide tanks in 1935.

boats were ordered from Yarwoods for the same work, but all steel, the first to be delivered in 1934 being the *Swallow* shown here. One of the principal chemicals carried for Courtaulds was the highly inflammable carbon disulphide and it was felt this could be better handled in large tanks rather than drums so in 1935 the boats were modified to take two long tanks each, butties as well as motors, with seacocks to flood the hold in case of fire. Surprisingly with such a dangerous cargo the motors had Gardner semi-diesel engines which depended on a blowlamp start! Decoratively the company favoured elaborate scrollwork and bold lettering. Whereas the butties were given family names the new motors were called after birds beginning with

'S' and bore a brass cut-out of the bird on the cabin side. Traffic declined after the Second War and many boats were turned over to coal. The carbon disulphide traffic ceased in 1951 and Cowburn & Cowpar gave up all canal transport in 1956.

Rescue of members of the Thomas Clayton fleet has been pretty successful over the last thirty years and two well-known ones are illustrated. The *Gifford* built by Nursers of Braunston in 1926 lasted until the end of Clayton's canal operations in 1966, latterly on the B.C.N. on short haul work, up to 1963 with a horse. In 1966 she was bought by Max Sinclair of Worcester and then passed to Martin Bunford of Shebdon. Both had kept her as she was and when I secured her in 1970 it was with a view to restoring her to the Clayton splendour which she deserved. This was at the start of the movement towards the Boat Museum, eventually established at Ellesmere Port where she still remains as a major exhibit. Extensive docking by Ken Keay came first, with paintwork by Tony Lewery, and since 1973 she has attended numerous waterway events. The *Gifford* incidently had worked with the *Dove* from Stanlow to Langley

Green, Oldbury, with fuel oil and with the *Tweed* from Oxford gasworks to the tar distillery at Banbury.

Claytons tried a utility style of lettering after the war, in the late 1950s and early 60s, for cheapness one assumes, and a few motors were so painted but not for long. For the company's last few years a return was made to the full glory of the Clayton cabin side, except for the *Spey* and the *Tay* which continued with T.C.(O) Ltd. to the end. The *Tay* was built by Fellows Morton & Clayton at Uxbridge in 1938, wooden like almost all of Clayton's fleet.

Above: A pair of Clayton horseboats, *Erne* and *Blyth*, in one of the Shropshire Union wide locks in the 1940s.

Left: Butty *Frome* working up Wolverhampton Locks about 1950, probably with oil from Ellesmere Port.

Latter Day Carriers

Carrying continued into the early 1970s due to the enterprise of a small group of operators trying to find profitable traffics. The Birmingham & Midland Canal Carrying Company was founded in 1965 and attracted much interest with a fleet quickly formed and established at Gas Street basin in Birmingham. Several traffics were begun: aluminium, timber, tomato purée, coal and most ambitious, in 1970, lubricating oil in special rectangular tanks, four to each boat. *Yeoford* and *Pictor* were so fitted and took oil from Ellesmere Port to Duckham's blending plant at Aldridge on the Daw End branch of the Wyrley & Essington, but after a number of trips the problems of canal depth ended the enterprise. Today Birmingham & Midland are busy with camping, passenger trips and commercial work and the *Yeoford* built by Yarwoods in 1937 for the Grand Union is still in service, albeit without the tanks.

Right: Anderton C. C. Co. boats *Mountbatten*, *Shad* and *Argo* at Preston Brook warehouses in 1969.

Below: *Yeoford* and *Pictor* winding at Aldridge on the B.C.N. after bringing a trial cargo of oil from Ellesmere Port in 1970.

A new Anderton Canal Carrying Co. was founded by Alan Galley and Jack Taylor in 1967 to take over the North Western business of Willow Wren with an office by the top of the Anderton Lift. A mixed fleet was built up, bought and hired from British Waterways. A variety of work began, aluminium to Wolverhampton, silicon carbide to Norbury near Stafford, feldspar to the Potteries, bentonite to Anderton and salt and bone meal to Preston Brook where a warehouse was leased. Salt for export was one of the final cargoes. The *Mountbatten* was one of the 'Admiral' class, a late effort by British Waterways to build a narrow boat with good carrying capacity, efficient covers for the cargo using hooped supports and battens and wedges along the gunwale, and roomier than usual accommodation which included a chemical toilet. *Mountbatten* was built in 1960 at Yarwoods at Northwich who built two pairs whilst another four came from Isaac Pimblott, also of Northwich.

Number Ones

The boats of the 'Number Ones', the captains who owned their own narrow boats personally, have long captured the imagination, mainly because of their lavish decoration coupled with their independence, although in economic terms they were no match for the bigger carrying companies and most had to sell out to them finally. Here are two well-known examples of boats owned by their captains. L.T.C. Rolt records meeting the Hones of Banbury in his book 'Narrow Boat' and D.J.Watkins-Pitchford illustrated two of their boats. The *Cylgate* was captained by the elder Alfred Hone whilst his son of the same name had the *White City* and the grand-daughters the *Rose and Betty*. Number Ones were not limited to one boat; a fleet among the family was more usual and on the Grand Junction they often worked in pairs behind a single big horse. Oxford

Decoration in progress by George Baxter on *Unostentatious* and *Philadelphius* in 1940 at Rickmansworth.

Canal Number Ones worked singly however carrying Warwickshire coal to destinations on the southern Oxford, in the case of the Hones to Banbury itself. The *Cylgate* was built of wood in 1930, probably by Sephton's of Tusses Bridge near Hawksbury. She remained with the Hones until 1946 when she was sold to Samuel Barlow who latterly paired her with the motor *Malta* until1959 when she was broken up. Barlow's acquired several boats from Number Ones unable to retain contracts in the face of undercutting by the bigger operators, notably the Grand Union Canal Carrying Company. Rolt remarks that Hone's *White City* carried a horse's tail at the ram's head and I have taken the liberty of transferring this to the *Cylgate*. (see also page 79)

Motor and butty pairs were introduced among the Number Ones by the late 1920s, conversions of horse boats at first, then new motors in the 1930s. They were expensive for a Number One and it was feared cargo space would be sacrificed, but this did not prove so serious. The *Unostentatious* was built in 1925, a wooden horse boat for Harold Canvin of Newton Locks near Leicester on the Old Union, almost certainly by Nurser's of Braunston because of the Daventry registration. In 1934 she was sold to Daniel Doughty, a Number One from Linslade, who paired her with the motor *Philadelphius* which he had acquired at the same time, also from Harold Canvin who carried up the Buckingham arm. Both were kept until 1940 when they were sold to Samuel Barlow. The *Unostentatious* became the *Nell* and the *Philadelphius* the *Dan*.

Decoration on both boats is lavish, particularly the application of diamonds. I'm not sure about those on the helm floats of the *Cylgate* but they do appear on the stern reconstruction of this boat at the National Waterways Museum at Gloucester which was prepared originally for the canal museum at Shardlow. Evidence for the *Unostentatious* appears in the *National Geographic Magazine* for August 1940.

Domestic and urban refuse was a common cargo well into the age of the motor dust cart and was indeed well suited to canal transport because of the high capacity of the boats compared with road vehicles. Local authorities ran their own fleets of refuse boats, although there were specialist rubbish carriers, notably Thomas Clayton of Paddington. The Birmingham Corporation narrow boat *No 17* was built in 1921 and remained in use into the 1950s, for Ken Keay remembered docking her then. The 131 on the top bend was her BCN number for toll purposes. For clarity I have enlarged the scroll work and the characteristic Keay decoration on the cabin doors. Note too the Keay docking date on the cabin waterway.

The *Swallow* was a wide boat like so many on the Regents Canal and the lower Grand Junction. She was built in 1923 for the St Marylebone Borough Council and passed to Thomas Clayton (Paddington) in 1939. Although her builder is not recorded she was certainly docked by Walkers of Rickmansworth and it is a photograph of her there which has provided evidence of her lettering, decoration and colour. She was one of some ten built for the council in the 1920s.

Salvage Department boats at work in Gas Street, Birmingham in the late 1950s.

Fly boats, introduced in the 1790s, operated on rivers and canals, both broad and narrow to provide express services for high value goods and perishables, either competing with or co-operating with fast light vans on the roads and later with rail. Fly boating meant travelling non-stop, day and night with double crews and relays of horse to ensure fast and regular deliveries. At locks they were given priority and could pass through them at night; they were allowed to overtake other craft and had right of way when meeting them, so special recognition symbols were needed.

On the Grand Junction, Pickfords put on narrow fly boats between Paddington, Manchester and Liverpool as soon as the canal was fully opened in 1805, later working from City Road basin on the Regent's Canal. They ran further fly boats from Birmingham to Leeds and to Stourport. Their boats sported a big red diamond on the cabin side. The Grand Junction Canal Company ran fly boats themselves but gave up in 1875 and their fleet was taken over and developed by what became Fellows Morton & Clayton who maintained an intensive service of steam fly boats from London to Braunston, Birmingham, Leicester, Nottingham and Derby. (see page 56)

Shropshire Union fly-boats were most probably developed as soon as the company started to carry in 1847, when placed under London & North Western Railway control. They covered the whole S.U. system

and more, converging on Ellesmere Port, not only the No 1 Fly from Birmingham and Wolverhampton but from the Potteries, Shrewsbury, Trench, Llangollen, and Newtown (Montgomeryshire), achieving remarkable schedules with their specially built boats with light loads of 15 to 18 tons. The boats carried a single black disc on

Above: Leeds and Liverpool company fly boats held up at Gargrave because of low water conditions, c.1910.

the top bend forward, the 'eyes' of a Shropshire Union boat. Anderton Company fly boats ran an express crated ware service from the Potteries to Runcorn and carried two red roundels (ordinary boats only had one.)

During the Second World War, and immediately after, the Grand Union Co. ran up to nine pairs running fly from Guinness' Park Royal brewery to Birmingham and back with empty barrels, the round trip taking a week.

Fly services by the Leeds & Liverpool Canal Co. dated back to about 1848, the year the company started carrying. When steamers came in 1880 they were put on fly work towing the former horse boats to make full use of their tireless machinery and limited cargo capacity. Fly boats, both steam and motor, continued under their successors Canal Transport and were clearly lettered 'FLY BOAT' on the fore end. On the river navigations the Aire & Calder were running fly boats from 1821 between Leeds and Selby to connect with steamers on the Ouse. With steam towage their fly services became more extensive, between the Humber and Leeds, Wakefield and Barnsley, the boats being lettered 'A.C.N. LICENCED FLY BOAT'.

John Dickinson was a papermaker who, in partnership with George Longman, formed a company in 1809 which was to become one of the most important customers of the Grand Junction Canal throughout its commercial life. It grew quickly and by 1830 there were five mills in Hertfordshire, all of them dependent on water power and all accessible to canal transport by linking water channels, with Apsley and Nash mills sited on the diverted line of the Grand Junction. Raw materials came up from London – esparto grass and woodpulp in from the docks whilst rags, waste paper and wood shavings were gathered into Dickinson's depot at Paddington, but all came up to the mills by the Grand Junction. The finished products were carried to London by an express narrow boat service, first to Paddington, later from 1930 to a depot on the Regent's near Kings Cross. From October 1890, Fellows, Morton & Clayton ran this contract, with steamers in full charge from 1897 to 1927 when motor boats took over. One round trip a day was achieved, totalling some 16 hours, 35 miles and 23 locks in each direction.

Two pairs and their crews were fully employed, Fellows, Morton & Clayton owned boats but painted in Dickenson's livery colours, the brown and gold seen on their road vehicles. The steamers used were the *Countess* and the *Princess*, the motors the *Jackal* and *Jaguar* both new in 1927. The *Kate* and *Alice* of 1910 were replacements for the butties *Maud* and *May* and were in their turn replaced in the 1930s by the *Yardley* and *Yiewsley*. The boats on this exacting work were called not surprisingly the Paper Mill Dashers, or more prosaically, the Paper Mill Boats. They ran up to 1939. Dickinson's had their own boats too, one motor for the Paddington run, several cabinless wide boats for internal mill traffic with which Fellows, Morton & Clayton helped out, as they did with the bringing up of raw materials. In 1934 Fellows, Morton & Clayton built a motor wide boat *Pioneer* for the paper dashing but she proved too slow and was soon withdrawn.

Coal was the other canal borne traffic. It was brought to all the mills when they changed from water to steam power and came from the Warwickshire field. Various carriers held contracts, Samuel Barlow, S.E. Barlow, The Grand Union Canal Carrying Company and British Waterways. But by the 1960s coal needs were much reduced, although Croxley took coal until September 1970, one of the last traffics on the Grand Union.

A pair of Dickinson's 'paper dashers' at work, 1930s.

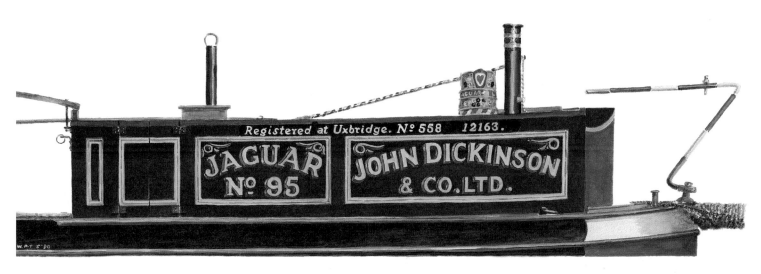

On the Basingstoke

Alexander John Harmsworth's family had been carriers on the Basingstoke Canal since the 1840s and in 1923 he bought the canal itself and his descendants continued to carry until 1949. They had a mixed fleet of barges and narrow boats, the latter useful for lightening their bigger Wey barges and for local work. Among the narrow boats were two, the *Greywell* and *Mapledurwell*, built in 1912 at Uxbridge by Fellows, Morton & Clayton for A. J. Harmsworth to a design suitable for the Thames tideway on which they worked tightly breasted up down to London docks behind a steam tug. Their stems were straight, they had washboards around the foredeck and an anchor windlass forward. They had neither cratch nor top planks but a normal pattern of towing mast and the cargo sheeted over and held by lashings to the gunwale rings. Decoration was lavish in respect of diamonds but neither roses nor castles were applied. They remained in service until 1939 when they were sunk at Ash Vale where their remnants remain.

Military stores to Aldershot, flour and timber were principal cargoes and during the 1914-18 war military stores were also handled by boats controlled by the War Office and manned by the Royal Engineers. Their decoration was more subdued than Mr Harmsworth's. After the war he acquired three of them which had come from Birmingham, as lightening boats and I have drawn the *Netherton* which must have been a typical BCN day boat although I am afraid her number is fictitious. Note on the *Greywell* the Cambridge blue on the top bend; Mr Harmsworth was a light blue supporter at the Boat Race.

Harmsworth boats at Ash Vale on the Basingstoke Canal, 1920s.

The early Bridgewater Canal Company pursued an energetic commercial policy, buying out the Mersey & Irwell competition in 1844 and competing strongly with the railways. Initially the canal held up well against goods and even passenger trains, but the 1840s were difficult years and eventually the Bridgewater came under railway control in 1872. A new Bridgewater Navigation Company was formed and a forward looking man, Edward Leader Williams, became general manager and engineer, determined to improve traffic flow by mechanical haulage. Cables were tried but steam screw tugs were adopted, although they meant a programme of bank walling. The Bridgewater had long had tugs on the Mersey but the 'little packets' introduced from 1875 were of special design for the canal.

All except one were built of Low Moor iron and twenty-six were eventually in service. The exception was the wooden *Runcorn* built at their own Old Quay Yard, Runcorn. The others came from Richard Smith at Preston and Edward Hayes of Stony Stratford on the Buckingham Branch of the Grand Junction, an isolated but busy shipyard founded by an agricultural engineer. They differed a little

Bridgewater Canal 'little packet' tugs at the coaling-up wharf in Runcorn, c.1920.

in size and shape, from 59ft to 61ft in length and from 7ft 7in to 8ft 9in in beam, and were not therefore narrow tugs in the strict sense. Their sterns varied too, bluntly pointed, round, rounded but squared off like the *Latchford* here, built in 1879 (registered Runcorn 438). Their general layout was similar and all had wheel steering. Boilers were of locomotive type and the engines single cylinder, 12in bore by 16in stroke and for this reason set fore and aft so the drive to the 36in diameter screw was by bevel gears. They were named after places on the Bridgewater or places linked to it by water, the lettering at the bow surrounded by scrollwork but kept plain at the stern. The two white bands on the funnel were inherited from the Duke's trustees and passed on to the Manchester Ship Canal Company. 200 rpm was the standard engine speed with boiler pressure at 80lbs per square inch. They were 'puffers' with no condenser and drew feed water from overside. The coal was stowed in bunkers each side of the boiler.

In 1887 the infant M.S.C.Co. bought the company because it needed the Mersey & Irwell channel but the Bridgewater Canal continued to provide welcome revenue then and for several decades to come. The 'Duker' tugs, sometimes called the 'little packets,' divided their time between the Bridgewater where they could manage four flats, and the Manchester Ship Canal where they could tow six in two columns of three with the wash passing between. The long cabin gave ample space for the three crew, captain, engineer and lad, which they needed since they were on duty day and night for a week at a time. In c. 1926 the *Stockton* was given a 50hp Widdop semi-diesel as an experiment. It was successful and 18 more tugs were dieselised whilst the remainder were scrapped. Under motor power the 'little packets' gained a new life into the 1950s and one, the *Lymm*, which became Richard Abel's *Dovedale*, worked to the late 1960s. Their appearance altered, the *Latchford* and her sisters now had a small funnel amidships while from 1939, cream

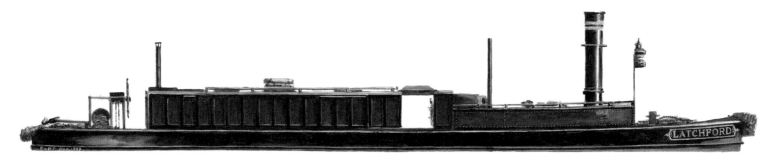

cabin sides framed in green replaced the old red and black colours and the slogan 'USE INLAND WATERWAYS' adorned what had been a boiler casing.

Although a wide canal, what became the Bridgewater Department of the M.S.C.C. kept a small fleet of narrow boats for a scheduled Runcorn-Manchester service, about ten in the 1920s, six by 1939 when they gave it up. They carried market produce, perishables, parcels, furniture and leather, with daily 1pm departures from the Town Warehouse, Runcorn Top Locks to Manchester calling at wharves along the way. Boats used, all horse-drawn, were the *Rover* of 1879 (registered Runcorn 513), the *Stream, Wave, Cyril, Dorothy, Produce, Minnow* and the *Duchess Countess*, which still carried some passengers between Knott Mill Manchester and Stockton Heath.

She remained in traffic to about 1924. In 1946/7 the service was resumed for a short while by Fellows, Morton & Clayton.

As a contrast to more exotic craft, here are a couple of plain ones, severely plain in the case of the Great Western boat. Both were used on the boatage services run by the railway companies on the Wolverhampton and Birmingham area canals to their canal/rail interchange basins, of which the GWR had ten and the London Midland & Scottish sixteen, thirteen inherited from the London & North Western and three from the Midland. The *Cheops* was built in 1889 for the Shropshire Union who ran boatage services for the L.N.W.R. and from 1895 was based at Brierly Hill, passing to the railway when the S.U. gave up carrying in 1921. The *Hockley* was first gauged in 1895 and was based at Hockley. These railway-run boats carried manufactured goods including food and drink products, castings and forgings, often moving at a trot. Some continued into nationalisation; on the Staffordshire & Worcestershire until November 1950, in the Birmingham area until April 1954.

Railway interchange boats at Hockley Port, Birmingham, 1912.

The arrival of the oil engine on the cut revolutionised B.C.N. traffic. There had been a few steam tugs, but 1919 heralded the motor tug for general towage, although there were already some motor tunnel tugs; in 1914 they were put on at Dudley and Gosty Hill. These were double-ended craft with a propeller at each end which was engaged by a clutch. The Dudley tug was called *George I*, the Gosty Hill *George II*, but the Dudley one had to be withdrawn because of lack of ventilation. The *George II* was sold in 1935 to C. W. Mitchard the Tipton coal merchant and converted by Peter Keay into a conventional tug. She was re-named *Jubilee* in that Silver Jubilee year. The conversion included removal of the bow propeller and the closing up of the aperture. Peter Keay's yard did a good deal of such work. His own *The Dart* had been a full length horse boat while the *Tiptonian*, a tug he converted for W. Elwell the coal

merchant had been a 'Rowley ragger' in quarry traffic. He also built some tugs from scratch, the *Progress* for Elwells and the *Judith Ann* for his own use. Tugs varied in length from the full seventy feet of Element's *Princess Anne*, formerly the Grand Union *Plato*, to the forty five feet of *Joan II* built by Worseys of Walsall in 1947 for Leonard Leigh of Hockley Port, a considerable firm of steerers and tug owners.

Above: *Princess Anne* at Bumblehole Junction.

Left: Mitchard's tug *Jubilee* after conversion from tunnel tug *George II* in 1935.

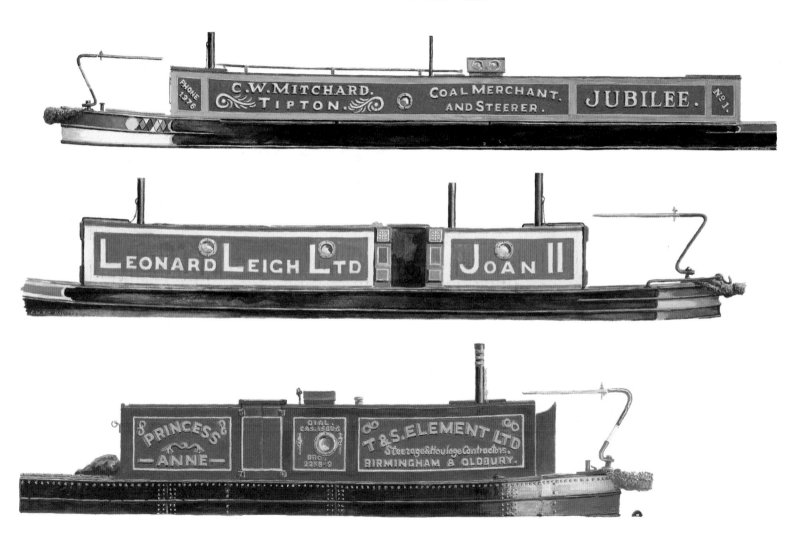

Here are three more tugs from the B.C.N. including the *Stentor* which, along with the *Hector*, were the first general towage motor tugs on the Birmingham system. They were built in 1919 for Chance & Hunt, the chemical manufacturers of Oldbury, by W.H.Walker & Brothers Ltd. of Rickmansworth, sub-contracting for James Pollock of Faversham, the Bolinder agents in Great Britain. Both were of course powered by Bolinder semi-diesels, designed to tow trains of day boats including liquid carriers.

During the Second World War, Stewarts & Lloyds acquired six pairs of narrow boats from the Grand Union Canal Carrying Co. which were used by their Stanton & Staveley subsidiary. The Stewarts & Lloyds *Tug No.2* shown here was one of them, shortened from the steel composite motor boat *Angol*, built in 1935 by Harland & Wolff. They also converted the *Vesta*, another 1935 'small

Woolwich', into a tug which became *Tug No.3*. The conversions were done by Harris's of Netherton in the 1950s. Harris also built the *Governor* for Yates Bros of Norton Canes but she was sold by them to Alfred Matty of Coseley who used her for both towage and pleasure trips. Latterly Mattys adopted a yellow livery, but I prefer the maroon.

Above: A train of empty B.C.N. coal boats on tow with a tug in July 1959, en route to becoming lightening boats for the Basingstoke Canal.

Left: Tug Stentor photographed after her launch at Walker Bros' yard at Rickmansworth in 1919.

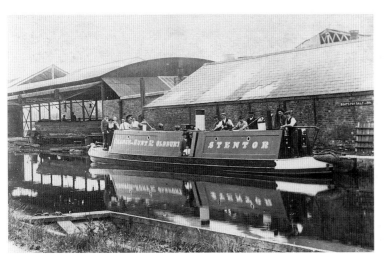

The 'Back of the Map' is the Black Country boatman's name for the canals on the SW side of Dudley and Netherton tunnels. Noah Hingley's forge was by the Dudley Canal at Netherton and relied on canal transport to carry away their products – anchors, chains, forgings and castings. 1921 saw their main carriers the Shropshire Union give up, leaving Noah Hingley and other Black Country forgemasters to the mercy of a railway monopoly and consequent high charges. The solution was to create their own canal carrying company which was done as quickly as possible when in 1922 Midlands & Coast Canal Carriers Ltd. was founded to work between the B.C.N. and the Mersey at Ellesmere Port. (see Page 23) Hingleys put their own long distance boats at the disposal of the company and new boats were ordered from the Dee shipbuilders Chrichtons of Saltney near Chester, and Yarwoods of Northwich. The *Jubilee* shown here was built by Yarwoods in 1927 as the *Leo*, a steel sided horse boat with elm bottoms. In 1935 she was converted into a motor and renamed *Jubilee* in honour of King George V and Queen Mary. In 1938 the Midlands & Coast fleet passed to Fellows, Morton & Clayton who continued the Black Country-Ellesmere Port traffic,

while *Jubilee* herself went in 1941 to Ernest Thomas of Walsall, a great acquirer of second hand tonnage.

Another of the new Midland & Coast boats from Yarwoods was the 1926 *North* which was withdrawn in 1937 and shortened and converted by Harris's of Netherton into a forty-four foot tug for Hingley's use. She was renamed *Crown*, an allusion to their trademark and the opportunity was taken to advertise the company's products on the usefully long cabin sides. The Staffordshire knot reminds us that Netherton was in Staffordshire.

Above: B.C.N. tug towing three loaded coal boats from Hednesford on the Cannock Extension Canal in the 1950s.

Left: Tug *Progress*, built for Elwell & Brown by Peter Keay's dock in the 1930s.

Whereas tug work on the narrow canals eventually centred on the B.C.N., the pioneers started elsewhere. In the 1840s steam tugs were put on the long pounds of the Macclesfield and the Birmingham & Liverpool Junction, although the Shropshire Union soon removed them from the latter. Another pioneer was *Pioneer*, a colliery owned tug on the Ashby which started work in 1856, while twenty years later the Sharpness New Docks Co. introduced steam tugs on the Worcester & Birmingham for tunnel work on the top pound and for ice breaking. From 1908 the steamers were replaced by three motor tugs, the *Sharpness*, *Worcester* and *Birmingham*. All were built by Isaac J. Abdela & Mitchell, *Sharpness* in 1908 at Brimscombe on the Thames & Severn Canal, the others in 1912 at Queensferry. The 48ft *Worcester* started life with a Kromhout twin cylinder semi-diesel but in 1930 was re-engined with a 30bhp Bolinder which she still retains. She lasted in service until 1956 and was used also on the Severn and in Gloucester Docks. In 1959 she was sold for scrap but was secured for preservation by the late Philip Murray, and his

executors gave her to what is now the Boat Museum at Ellesmere Port. Her triumphant restoration has been based on the description by George Bate of the Tardebigge workshops, a red hull and a black funnel with the white band of the Sharpness New Docks Co., edged by red bands, which may have been an early variant worn by company boats on the Worcester & Birmingham, for photographs after 1930 show no funnel bands at all.

Above: Steam tunnel tug, Number 1 or 2, waiting at the south end of Preston Brook tunnel on the Trent and Mersey Canal c. 1940.

Left: Tug *Worcester* pulling a train of narrow boats through the docks at Gloucester in c. 1930.

Also at Ellesmere Port awaiting restoration is the 25ft long motor tug *Beeston* built by Yarwoods at Northwich for the London, Midland & Scottish Railway in 1946 for maintenance work and ice-breaking, and fitted latterly with an Armstrong Siddeley diesel. Her cabin had a stove and two berths and doubled as a wheelhouse, more sheltered than a tiller at the stern. The one illustrated was for emergency use.

To a smaller scale is one of the Preston Brook, Barnton and Saltersford tunnel tugs from the Trent & Mersey Canal, *Number 1* or *2*, possibly introduced in 1864 when the towing service commenced. They were 56ft long by 7ft beam and were equipped with spring loaded guide wheels to save steering. In 1910 they were joined by a larger and deeper tug, *Number 3*, 60 feet long by 9 ft 6 in beam which could only work through Preston Brook. Tunnel towage lasted until the 1940s by which time most of the boats were motor and butty pairs.

Most carrying companies developed their own individual patterns or insignia for the bows of their craft as part of their company livery, and most seem to start from a simple painted section that echoes the tapering shape of the top strake of a wooden boat where it tips in and up to the stempost. If it is a dark shape it will be contrasted with a light border, most commonly red surrounded by a white outline. That shape in turn may carry a further design, diamonds, crescents or more painted roses but the commonest ingredient by far is a simple circle. This is so like the iris of an eye that one wonders whether there is any tenuous connection, conscious or otherwise, to the ancient 'oculus' tradition of painting the eye of the Goddess Osiris on the bow so the ship can see its way ahead.

Opposite page;
Top left is the stem of one of the Yarwood built composite motor boats built in 1933 for Cowburn & Cowpar of Manchester, either the *Swan* or the *Swift* whose printed painting specification has been followed. (see page 97)

Lower left is the later Mersey-Weaver colour scheme, taken from a 1956 photo of the ex-Anderton Co. *Spain*. Earlier Anderton and Mersey-Weaver fore ends were plain white. (see page 27)

Top right is the Cowburn & Cowpar horse boat *Ivy*. She was docked, it is thought, by Lees & Atkins at Polesworth and Polesworth roses enhance the fore cabin side. (see page 97)

Centre right is a six plank Runcorn boat owned by Jonathon Horsefield with a straightish stem. (see page 43)

Lower right is the later Anderton Company colour scheme. (see page 25)

Above: Cowburn & Cowpar's *Ivy*, resplendent with diamonds on every available stand and upright, poses for a photograph on the Bridgewater canal in 1930.

Right: Motor boat *Swan* or *Swift*, new at Yarwoods in Northwich in 1933.

Some canal and river authorities stipulated that the boat's name should be clearly marked at both bow and stern and most of these southern fleet liveries follow that instruction.

Top left is the *Redshank* of Willow Wren, a steel motor which started life in 1936 as the Grand Union's *Reading*, a Large Northwich. (see page 51)

Lower left: In 1949 British Waterways reversed their colour scheme with azure blue predominating. The Large Woolwich steel motor *Coleshill* of 1937 was so painted for the 1950 Festival at Market Harborough along with the butty *Ayr*. (see page 67)

Top right: Built in 1935 the wooden motor *Electra* came from Walkers of Rickmansworth and was paired with the *Ethiopia* in the Grand Union fleet. Note the upswept Ricky stem and the early Grand Union colours. (see page 53)

Centre right: The steel motor *Southall* was built by Yarwood's at Northwich in 1937 for the Grand Union and is here shown in Coronation colours of that year. (see page 53)

Lower right: Initially in 1948 British Waterway's colours were predominantly yellow, and the steel 'Royalty' class motor *Henry* was, according to the specification preserved at the museum in Gloucester, so painted. She was built by Pollocks at Faversham. (see page 67)

Willow Wren's *Quail* and *Dunlin* heading south on the North Oxford near Braunston in July 1961.

Narrow boat cabins were decorated in contrasting colours at their rear for easy recognition, especially on the Birmingham Canal Navigations, as one approached them end-on by water or along the towpath. Added to the colours were the patterns, of particular value on the Birmingham system. The patterns here are of long distance boats and some have recognised the designs as akin to those on carts or wagons. The thirteen shown here are a selection from motor boats and butties, plus a steamer.

1. From about 1949 the Anderton Company design changed to this; earlier backs were probably black & white. (see page 25)

2. Later Mersey Weaver cabin rear design, dating from the early 1940s. Earlier ones were also most probably black & white. (see page 27)

3. Fellows, Morton & Clayton went over to red and green in the mid 1920s with this pattern of cabin back. (see page 59)

4. Shropshire Union boats relieved their bold black and white with blue. (see page 35)

5. Fellows, Morton & Clayton steamers, as can be seen on the *President* today, carried the black & white round to the cabin back. (see page 57)

6. Severn & Canal boats used a dark blue livery, sometimes dispensing with any pattern at all at the rear. (see page 63)

7. Willow Wren adopted a traditional shape. (see page 51)

8. Tradition was abandoned by the Grand Union Canal Carrying Company who simply picked out the cabin shape, in this case in the 1937 Coronation colours, red, white and blue. (see page 53)

9. British Waterways in their first year, 1948, followed the Grand Union shape with their novel and unpopular colours. (see page 67)

10. Some companies adopted a variant to the traditional curves, for example Thomas Clayton. Their *Gifford* was so painted. (see page 91)

11. Cowburn & Cowpar carried their maroon cabin side colour round to the back. (see page 97)

12. Earlier Grand Union colours were light and dark blue; the change came in 1937. (see page 53)

13. Back to British Waterways who in 1949 reversed their colours to make azure blue predominant. Some boats such as the *Southam* in 1956 appeared with this modification. (see page 71)

1.

2.

3.

British Waterways' boats at
Nash Mills, Apsley on the
Grand Union in May 1956.

4.

5.

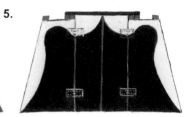

6.

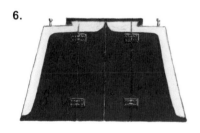

7.

8.

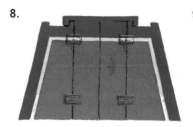

9.

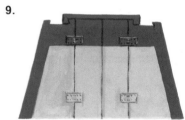

10.

11.

12.

13.

Disliked by boat people and by the health authorities, narrow boat fore cabins came as a result of space requirements laid down by the *Canal Boats Acts* of 1877 and 1884. Children were packed into these hutches, just over 6ft long, narrowing forward and constantly damped by leaking lock gates. They had a cross bed and a side bed and were warmed by a bottle stove.

Top left: Many of the Shropshire Union fleet were fitted with fore cabins, were 'two decked boats' as the boatmen called them. In slim built boats requiring the full length of the hold for cargo they were very small indeed. (see page 35)

Lower left: The *Princess* was a little bigger, a 'Royalty' class wooden butty built in 1931 by Bushell Brothers of Tring to go with the Pollock built steel motor *Prince*. Here she is in the colours of

Associated Canal Carriers, whom the Grand Union bought in 1930 and renamed The Grand Union Canal Carrying Co. Ltd. in 1934. (see page 51)

Top right: The largest narrow boat fore cabins were those in tankers, making use of all the buoyancy space forward of the fixed liquid-proof bulkhead. The Thomas Clayton tar boat *Gifford*, built by Nursers of Braunston in 1926, is one of those with a fore cabin today. She is preserved at the Boat Museum Ellesmere Port. (see page 91)

Lower right: The wide boat *Golden Spray* was built in 1922 by Bushell Brothers of Tring for T.W.Toovey, the King's Langley flour millers and her fore cabin had the bonus of a little extra width. (see page 79)

F.M.& C. fore cabin boats seen here at Braunston during a strike in 1923.

Royalty class butty *Albert* outside Bushell Bros dock at Tring, perhaps just newly launched in 1931.

Maintenance Boats

Not over decorative, but essential to waterway life is the maintenance fleet. It had many duties and it is only possible to illustrate a selection of craft which ranged from heavy dredgers to punts carrying hedge trimmings. Many were former carrying boats downgraded to transport tools and materials and act as mess rooms, and some were converted into simple spoon dredgers. One of these is illustrated, taken from a well-known photograph of a dramatic burst at Marbury near Northwich on the Trent & Mersey in 1907. A maintenance boat lies at the bottom of the hole. She carries the Staffordshire knot badge of the North Staffordshire Railway, the 'Knotty', owners of the canal since 1847 who looked after it well and worked it hard as a valuable extension of their close-knit railway system. Her cabin side colours are frankly guessed – the railway livery was crimson and the dark tone of the photograph makes crimson a possibility. They certainly had a spoon dredger called the *Oregon*. These were worked by two men, one at the windlass, the other handling the spoon or scoop which had a capacity of half

a hundred-weight. Although slow these dredgers had the advantage of being able to dig in awkward corners and carried their own spoil away, and the type remained in use on canals into the mid-twentieth century.

The other pictures show the cabins of narrow work boats from other railway owned canals. From 1846 the Shropshire Union came under the control of the L.N.W.R., and like the North Staffs was handed over to the L.M.S. in 1923. The *Severn* was employed on the Montgomeryshire section of the Shropshire Union and bears a similar livery to their carrying boats. Her fleet number is fictitious as the real one cannot be found.

The London & North Eastern Railway boat *Henry* worked on the Macclesfield, a canal the L.N.E.R. inherited from the Great Central, whose predecessors acquired it in 1846. She was painted brown and her cabin was extended for use as a mess room. There were many other specialist craft like pump boats for emptying lock chambers and tunnels, tunnel inspection boats with staging and lights, pile driving boats for bank protection, floating forges and carpenters' boats but there is insufficient space to show more.

Above: The dredger *Joan*, thought to be seen here on the Macclesfield Canal in the 1920s.

Left: General maintenance boat *Joel* working through lock 17 on the Ashton Canal in 1936.

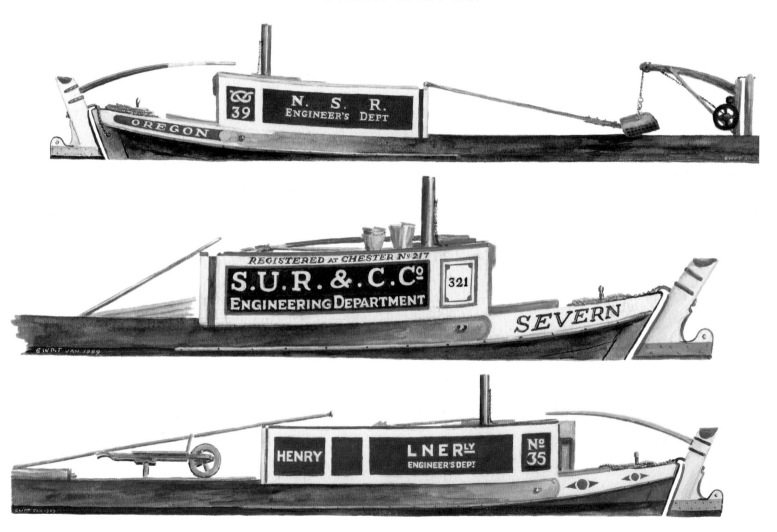

Leeds and Liverpool

Leeds & Liverpool Canal boats were built in two sizes, 60 feet in length if trading the full distance of the canal, 72 feet if limited to Liverpool, Wigan, Leigh and the Bridgewater Canal. There were plenty of both, the short boats carrying up to 40 tons of coal on a draught of 3 ft 6 in, the long 70 tons on a draught of 5 feet or so. Many of the horse boats were square sterned, although the Leeds & Liverpool Canal Co's own fly-boats kept the rounded or pointed stern. Principal accommodation was aft in the horse boats with more spartan living space forward. However when the steam fly-boats were introduced in 1880, all the accommodation had to move forward.

Cargo protection was by cloths spread over three rails held up by forked stanchions and the horses hauled from masts stepped either on the centre line in a lutchet like a keel's, or to one side or the other depending where the towpath was. The centre mast was normally kept for lock work although fly-boats generally used it at all times. This central mast was retained by steam and motor boats.

Decoration followed a tradition of its own, but the object was the same as in the narrow boats, to brighten up what was for many the family home. Scrolls, geometric design, floral patterns and the occasional cottage or castle were the principal motifs, particularly on the square sterns which allowed plenty of scope. Great attention was paid to bold heavily shaded lettering. Whereas some carriers encouraged lavish

A transom stern horsedrawn short boat at Lydiate on the Leeds and Liverpool canal, c. 1920

decoration others favoured a more modest style. The Canal Company itself only painted their initials on the stern with the boat's name on the boiler and engine room casing. The steamer *William Robinson* became No 30 in the company's carrying fleet which had started in 1848. Their horse boats were more ornate with scroll work at stem and stern, red, blue and green being favoured colours.

Like the Shropshire Union, the Leeds & Liverpool gave up carrying in 1921 but re-entered it in 1930 by amalgamating three carriers and a warehousing company into Canal Transport Ltd. One of the constituents was Ben C. Wall of Skipton the former canal company's inspector who had commenced carrying on his own in 1921 when the company gave up. His boats were named after planets and letters of the Greek alphabet and bore the modest decoration illustrated by the motor boat *Psi* built in 1928. Motors had been introduced to the Leeds & Liverpool in 1924 by Ben Wall and many horse boats were converted, including *Murillo* built in 1913 and converted in 1955. Like most of John Parke's of Bankhall, Liverpool, fleet she was a 72 footer, for the company concentrated on the Wigan-Liverpool coal trade. Red was the Parke's colour and most of their names ended in 'O'.

They remained in business until 1964, latterly under British Waterways administration. Another long-lived Liverpool carrier was Richard Williams who continued until 1961, delivering coal to Tate & Lyles. Some of his square sterned boats, mostly long ones, were magnificently embellished, notably the *Richard*. The horse boat *Tom* is more modest and features the red and blue scheme which was replaced by white with red, green and blue trimmings. Finally comes a Blackburn short boat, the motor *Marjory* owned by Crook & Thompson who were coal merchants. The black diamond is an obvious symbol, contrasting with the white diamond of T. Crook & Son also of Blackburn.

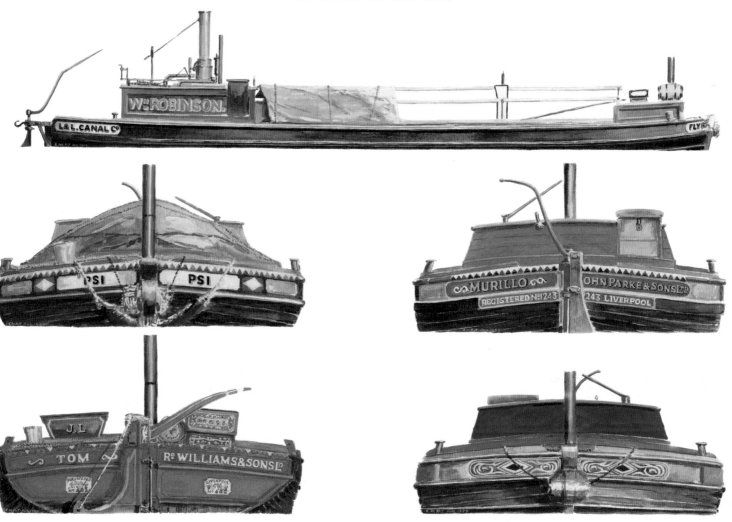

Grain from Birkenhead

Flour millers in Lancashire used the Leeds & Liverpool Canal to bring up grain and distribute flour. Two invested in a fleet of boats designed to cross the Mersey to load grain at Birkenhead. H.& R. Ainscough, of Burscough and Parbold, had a fleet of long wooden horse boats but in 1933 started to order steel motor and dumb barges from Yarwoods at Northwich. Eight were built, four motor and four dumb, although one of the dumb craft was lost in the Liverpool blitz in 1941, while an extra one was the horse boat *Parbold*. All were 72 feet long for they were not expected to use the short locks up from Wigan. The motor *Ambush* of 60 tons was paired with the dumb *Attractive*, both built in 1933. These names were taken from Ainscough's shire horses, the *Ambush* being registered at Liverpool No 1594. Her name as painted on the bow was distinctive, the work of the Forshaw brothers who crewed her for many years. Usually letters were plain white on the red hull.

Similar craft, but only 61 feet long for the short locks at Wigan, were the seven steel motor boats ordered by Ranks, again from Yarwoods, for their British Isles Transport subsidiary to take grain up to their Appleby mills at Blackburn. Like the Ainscough boats they could cross the Mersey, for they were given coamings and hatchboards like a ship, lifebuoys, navigation lights and a mast for a steaming light. Of 45 ton capacity the *A39* built in 1933 passed in 1949 to Henry Croasdale of Blackburn for local coal traffic. Renamed *Peace*, she later became a passenger trip boat, as did the *Ambush* which also carried coal for a while after 1961, the year Ainscoughs withdrew from canal operations.

Canal Transport Ltd., the 1930 amalgamation backed by the Leeds & Liverpool Canal Co., started a modest building programme in 1932 when they placed orders for steel motor short boats with W. J. Yarwood and Isaac Pimblott. Each delivered nine, named after rivers, and wooden

Above:
Claymore at the Rufford branch junction at Burscough in September 1958.

Left: Ainscough grain barges in Stanley Dock, Liverpool in 1956.

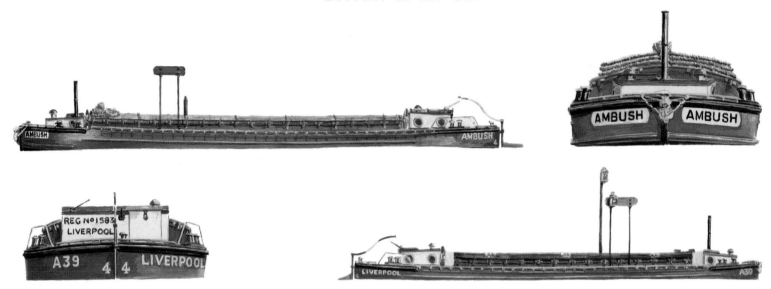

motor boats came from Mayor's of Wigan and Tarleton. The 45 ton capacity Yarwood *Ribble* of 1934 was registered No 1609 at Liverpool. Although not given coamings or hatch boards she and her sisters crossed the Mersey with their 18 hp Widdop engines. Her decoration is a toned down version of the Leeds and Liverpool

tradition, modest scroll and toothed patterns against a grey and white background with black and red trimmings. Surprisingly British Waterways continued the decorative tradition with the craft they added to the fleet, their last from Harland & Wolff in 1953.

Scroll Work

Leeds & Liverpool boat decoration achieved heights of lavishness at bow and stern, particularly on the transom of the square sterned boats. Scroll work was a main feature allied to frieze patterns, for example the toothed and rounded sequence along the cover board. The wooden short boat *Mary*, whose bow and stern are shown here, was last docked in about 1962 by T. & J. Hodson, the canal boat builders at Whitebirk, Blackburn. One of the boat builders was Sam Yates, who also did the signwriting, and the *Mary* was the last boat on which he worked. The *Mary* was built for Crook & Thompson, the carriers, in 1958-59 at Riley Green near Blackburn. She came under Hargreaves' ownership later, which explains the burning H on the rudder head. She remained at work into the mid-1960s.

Above: Bow decoration on Canal Transport's *Don* at New Lane, Burscough, c.1942.

Left: A pair of short boats with coal for Liverpool at Saracen's Head, Halsall in July 1956.

Lancaster Canal boats followed the Leeds & Liverpool style in design but the locks allowed them all to be 72 ft long by 14 ft 6 in beam with a 50 ton coal capacity. They were exclusively square sterned but did not use the space to the same decorative advantage as on the Leeds & Liverpool. Lancaster carriers favoured the boat's name in large letters and the use of motifs along the hull side at stem and stern. Dots and dashes were used by Baines Brothers of Preston, the last principal carriers, some of whose boats were taken over in 1941 by the Ashcroft family, mainly for the coal traffic to Storey's mill in Lancaster, which finished in 1947. The *Kenneth* was among the final boats employed and remained afloat at Catforth near Preston certainly until 1955.

A major Lancaster canal carrier was the Wigan Coal & Iron Company. They were colliery proprietors on a large scale, formed by amalgamation in 1865 out of, among others, the Kirklees Hall Coal & Iron Company. Controlled by the Crawford and Balcarres

family they also owned ironworks, mineral railways and seagoing colliers. In 1886 they had a total fleet of 70 canal boats, the majority on the Leeds & Liverpool where they employed steam tugs *England*, *Scotland* and *Wales* of 1871, the pioneers of steam on this canal. Their trademark was a star, displayed on their railway wagons and as a pattern on the sides and stern of their boats. On the Lancaster the name of the boat was in large letters.

Because of the few docks, wooden boats were rare on the Lancaster. Allsupp's of Preston built iron and steel ones but their

Above: *Express* loading coal under a wagon tippler at Preston basin about 1923.

Left: Empty Lancaster Canal coal boats at Preston basin during a coal strike in 1921.

Ribble yard had no canal link so they had to go round by sea to Glasson Dock. There were never any motor boats, just two Leeds & Liverpool steamers for a while in the 1930s, so horses were in charge. They hauled from a mast stepped to one side or the other depending on the towpath. The main accommodation was aft, a fairly roomy cabin entered by a companion and with a raised coach roof. Features of these boats were the two air vents aft, round holes closed by slides, while the water was kept in an iron tank with a tap. Many were family boats, with a plainer cabin forward for the mate or for the children.

Keels & Sloops

Among British inland craft no vessel is more distinctive than the sailing keel of the Humber with her square rig, a single masted full-rigged ship and always called a ship by her captain and crew. Much has been written about the Norse and Mediaeval ancestry of the rig, but it survived because of its practicality, ability to go to windward, spill wind, to reef, to sail in confined waters bounded by trees and buildings. For river and canal work the rig could not be bettered.

Within the keel family were many variants of hull size and sail plan, hull size being determined by the navigations for which the ship was intended, sail plan by the amount of tidal work likely to be undertaken. Many keels were not rigged (see page 139) so relied on horses and tugs, whilst others carried enough sail to make coastal passages although this was rare. While wooden keels were built up to about 1914, iron and steel keels were by then well-established and steel sailing keels continued to be delivered until the 1930s. They were given a wealth of mechanical aides for the two man crew, tack rollers forward, sheet rollers, halliard rollers and leeboard rollers aft. Leeboards were needed for going to windward but not all rigged keels had them. Standing and running rigging was mostly wire and easily dismantled when the mast had to be lowered or put ashore when going inland. The leeboards went ashore too and the horse marine or the tug took over. Most of the keels were owned on the Yorkshire side of the Humber and there were some big carriers like Furleys and Bleasdales.

Sloops were different in the sense that the rig was fore and aft but the hull was the same, and the same variants of hull dimensions for inland work applied to sloops as to keels. However, many tended to be larger and so restricted to the Humber estuary for which they were best suited. Indeed it was for Humber conditions that the rig was chosen, and much of their work depended on the estuary, gravel from Spurn, sand from Paull, sand and gravel from the Trent, chalk stone from Barton. Because many of their cargoes came from the Lincolnshire side– bricks, tiles, cement, farm produce – most sloops were owned on the south bank including the small market boats which went daily from Barton to Hull with vegetables.

Decoration of keels and sloops could be elaborate, the nature of this being left to the captain even if the ship belonged to a fleet. The hawse timbers or plates bore distinctive colours and the top strake might be in contrast to the rest of the hull. Blue and green were favoured by many, but Farleys of Hull stuck to their yellow, the Trent Navigation to white and John Hunt of Leeds to red. There was not much scope for embellishment in a steel keel or sloop, save for picking out timber heads, beading and rails in a contrasting colour, but in a wooden vessel there was room for carved and painted work on the stem chock between the hawse timbers in a short stemmed keel, on the featherings flanking the hawse timbers, and on the cross pieces between the hawse and long timbers. Decorative panels could be created by 'stringing' or lining out and the stayfall block chock was another piece of carved work. Its task was to hold the lower block of the stayfall tackle clear of the windlass when the mast was lowered.

All this information comes from two sources, Captain John Frank and Captain Fred Schofield and the keel illustrated is Captain Schofield's wooden *Guidance* of 1905 and the sloop Captain Frank's steel *Nero* of 1897, which he used in the brick trade from the family yard at Ferriby sluice on the Ancholme. The stem decoration of the *Guidance* is shown in detail and the stem colours of the two keel owners, Jonas Braithwaite of Hull who carried coal to Reckitts in Hull and Furleys who were founded in 1774. By the sloop *Nero* is a detail of her stem and below that the stem colours of John Richardson's steel sloop *Yokefleet* built for the Market Weighton Canal and Driffield Navigation.

Sheffield Keels

Sheffield size keels were many and varied, working under sail, steam and motor. Their 61 ft 6in length by 15 ft 6 in beam allowed them not only up the Sheffield & South Yorkshire and the Sheffield Canal but up the tidal Trent, the Aire & Calder and the Ouse, although they were too wide for the older Trent locks and too long for the Dearne & Dove Canal. Among the bigger owners on the Sheffield & South Yorkshire was William Bleasdale, working from Hull. He founded his business in the late nineteenth century and chose, like so many others, a blue colour scheme although his naming, with the 'cliffe' suffix, was readily distinguished. In the 1930s his wooden and steel keels (the *Southcliffe* built by Dunstons of Thorne in 1923 was one of the latter) were gradually replaced by steel motor craft which eventually came under the control of British Waterways.

Rishworth, Ingleby & Lofthouse of the Swan Flour Mills in Hull ran six steam keels, two of which, the *Swiftsure* of 1904 and the *Ril* were within Sheffield size and worked between Hull and Rotherham. The others, the *Swan, Eagle, Cygnet* and the *John M. Rishworth* were bigger. Spillers took over the mills between the wars and altered the painting of the hawse plates from green to diagonal red and white. These steamers, except the *Ril* and the *John M. Rishworth*, both of which had their wheel amidships, steered from aft and their funnels were hinged for the bridges.

Carrying today, Ernest Waddington of Swinton near Mexborough, have a big fleet including the *Heritage* built in 1962 at their Swinton dock. The company was founded in the 1820s and maintained a

fleet of horse hauled and sailing keels and sloops until diesels were introduced between the wars into craft which achieved capacities of up to a hundred tons. Coal, steel and grain were principal cargoes and the company's wharf at Eastwood, Rotherham, in use since the 1950s, has been extended. The Waddington coat of arms, incorporated into a flag, has been flown on special navigational occasions, like the open-ing of the enlarged locks on the Sheffield & South Yorkshire.

Opposite page above:
Humber sloop *John and Anne* unloading coal at Ferriby Sluice on the River Ancholme, date unknown.

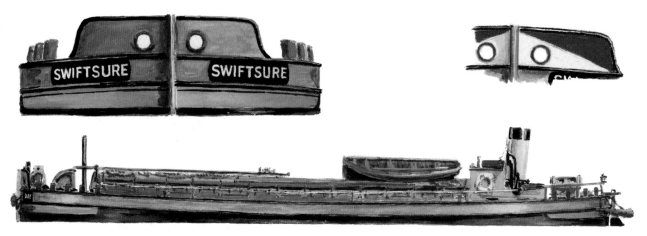

Also in the keel family were the 57 ft 6 in long tidal and non-tidal Yorkshire keels or 'West Country' boats, built for the short locks of the Calder & Hebble Navigation. The non-tidal keels were unrigged and without leeboards, the tidal ones, a foot less in hold depth than Humber keels, might be rigged like a keel with square mainsail, topsail and leeboards so could work out into the Humber safely which the non tidal keels could not. Both varieties could range over the West Riding system and, via the Rochdale, over the Pennines to Manchester and Liverpool. 60 tons on a 5 feet draught was their capacity although latterly the Rochdale admitted less than four feet.

Owners along the Calder & Hebble were numerous, not only carriers but manufacturers. One of the main carriers was Albert Wood of Sowerby Bridge who in 1894 bought two craft from the Rochdale Canal Company which had been owned by his former employers William Jackson & Sons of Manchester. They sold out to the Rochdale in 1891. Wood expanded his fleet and by the 1900s had 35 West Country boats, two Mersey 'cut' flats and thirteen narrow boats, mainly on the Ashton and Peak Forest. (see page 7) Wood kept the yellow colours of Jackson's and had his own dock at Shepley Bridge, Mirfield. Here in 1910 the *Eddie* was launched, a non-tidal Yorkshire keel, here seen in profile with the horse towing from the 'neddy' stepped in the lutchet. A stem view of the same craft shows the decorative details some of which are enlarged, the scroll work on the featherings either side of the hawse timbers, the stem chock which stiffened the timbers on the short stemmed craft

Keel *Eddie,* launched at Shepley Bridge dock on the Calder and Hebble Navigation for Albert Wood in 1910.

and the brass lamb on the stempost, a symbol of the Yorkshire woollen trade. Others sported a horse. In 1915 the *Eddie* was sold to L.B.Holiday, the Huddersfield chemicals firm and became the *Phenol*.

Also short stemmed but a tidal keel, capable of river and estuary work, was the *John* of the Calder Carrying Company, founded in 1908-9 by the Calder & Hebble proprietors to bring more traffic to

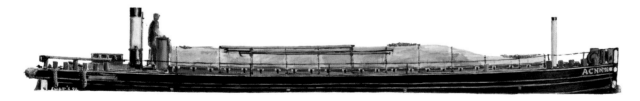

their system. Her stem chock bears the CCC monogram of the company. Another example of a tidal keel, long stemmed in this case, with a hold depth of 6 ft 6 in and loading to an inch short of five feet draught, was the *Carmine* of British Dyestuffs of Huddersfield who became a major component of ICI. Their boats were named after dyes, *Safranine* was another, while Holidays were named after chemicals.

Finally the stem of an Aire & Calder steam fly-boat, also illustrated in profile. These were carvel built wooden vessels, some 70 ft long by 14 ft 10 in beam. They ran between Humber Dock in Hull and Leeds and Wakefield so forming a link with the Calder & Hebble. They could also go up the Barnsley Canal. Latterly there were two, not to be confused with the 85 ft long iron merchandise tugs of the Aire & Calder which offered a regular towage service from Goole up to Leeds and Wakefield.

Yorkshire Tankers

Both companies here have played a major role in inland water transport; Harker's were pioneers in motor river and canal tanker craft operation and Whitaker's are in business today, running vessels on the Clyde, at Belfast, on the Tyne, Mersey, Manchester Ship Canal, Falmouth and Southampton as well as on their home waterways of Yorkshire. John Harker's business went back to the late nineteenth century when he carried for Stainsby & Lyon's Aire tar distillery at

Knottingley, founded in 1877. In 1918 the Harker fleet was bought by Stainsby & Lyon who added motor and dumb vessels carrying liquid in bulk. The first of their motor tankers appeared in 1925, loading oil and tar in bulk. Hitherto both had been carried in casks but experiment in bulk carriage by dumb craft had proved successful and Stainsby & Lyon were encouraged to expand. In 1926 they sold their tar distillery and concentrated on barge operation using the John Harker name. Two Knottingley shipyards were acquired in 1929, one at Gloucester in 1939 and another at Sharpness in 1946. In these they built and repaired for themselves and others. In 1948 they bought the Severn & Canal Carrying Company, retaining their tankers and by 1957 they had a hundred barges. The *Courtdale H*, built at Knottingley in 1958 was able to carry 270 tons of 'black oil' or boiler fuel oil, for which a steaming plant and so a funnel was needed. Other craft concentrated on refined petroleum products and had a greater carrying capacity since the cargo was lighter. They had no funnels, the engines exhausting over the stern to avoid sparks igniting fumes from the tanks. The *Courtdale H* which measured 138 feet in length was scrapped in 1974 and two years later Harkers started to run down their barge operations some of which were kept by Whitakers who retained the name.

John H. Whitaker (Holdings) Ltd. also commenced business in the late nineteenth century, in 1885, with two wooden craft and a sailing billyboy. Creosote was carried in double-skinned wooden tankers from 1907 and petroleum in drums from 1910. Bulk liquid carriage was started in the 1920s using dumb craft with the first motor tanker, the *Vincit,* coming in 1937. From 1917 the company

Left above: Harker's 250 ton spirit tanker *Lonsdale H* at the entrance to the Knottingley-Goole Canal in May 1957.

Left bottom: The 100 ton capacity tanker *Rienzi*, owned by Whitaker's, discharging at Ferrybridge on the Aire & Calder Navigation in 1973.

had two shipyards on the River Hull which they formed into the Yorkshire Dry Dock Co. Ltd., (Y.D.D.) Much expansion took place from about 1950 and by 1973 Whitaker's were employing 32 tankers and 11 dry cargo vessels. Subsequently craft were acquired from the Harker and Cory fleets and the company also entered the coasting tanker and dry cargo trades. The *Humber Mariner* was built by the Y.D.D. in May 1963 and was lengthened in 1970 to give a capacity of up to 350 tons of petroleum. The Whitfleet subsidiary with the blue livery is a 1970s foundation to carry petroleum from Immingham to the Fleet depot at Woodlesford near Leeds, on the Aire & Calder. The *Fleet Enterprise* was built in March 1983 by the Y.D.D. with a 700 ton capacity on a ten foot draught, limited to 550 tons on an eight foot draught permitted on the Aire & Calder.

Trent Navigation

Navigation of the Trent was hampered by shallowness and, until the improvements below Nottingham of the late 1920s, by small locks. Craft had to stay within a length of 81 ft and a breadth of 14 ft 6 in. The locks above Nottingham remained small and traffic was handled by Upper Trent boats, 60 ft long by 14 ft beam, miniature keels, with open holds of 40 to 50 tons capacity and a single square sail. From 1882 the Trent Navigation entered the carrying trade to encourage business, hiring craft like the Furley's Upper Trent boat illustrated, and buying tugs such as the *Little John* with twin screws working in tunnels because of the exceptional shallowness, as little as twenty inches in the 1880s. More progress was made from 1896 under the energetic Frank Rayner with keels built at the Navigation's dock at Newark and other craft ordered from the Watson shipyard at Beckingham opposite Gainsborough. Traffic below Nottingham was in the hands of larger keels, The Trent version was the 'catch' or ketch, longer at 74 ft than most keels to take advantage of the 82 ft 6 in locks, but restricted to 14 ft 6 in breadth in the 14 ft 9 in wide chambers. Catches were sharper fore and aft than a keel and were square bilged. The standing lug mizzen which gave the ketch appearance was not universal although it was general to have a wide foot to the mainsail to provide added power. Illustrated is the *Brothers* of 1887, owned by Captain James Gardiner of Hull. She had a hold depth of six feet and a capacity of 120 tons on a 5 ft 6 in draught if the river allowed it which until

Tug *Riverman* and keels on the Trent at Keadby, undated but probably 1930s.

the 1920s it did not. There is a portrait of the *Brothers* in the Town Docks Museum, Hull by Reuben Chappell.

Decoration of these craft was not remarkable but followed keel practice. (see page 135) Between 1887 and 1892 Trent Navigation craft carried the long-winded title 'Trent Burton-

on-Trent and Humber Navigation Co.' cut into the top strake of the stern, while hawse timbers, hawse plates, top strakes and timber heads were later picked out in the red and white that the Trent Navigation chose for its carrying fleet, along with red coamings and a red stern rail.

1929 saw the completion of the 180 ft by 29 ft locks below Nottingham and with the extensive dredging the Trent Navigation started a fleet modernisation programme for the traffic between Nottingham and the Humber ports. There was still a narrow Newark Town Lock and a narrow flood lock at Holm, the former not enlarged until 1952 and the latter not eliminated until 1954, so the steel motor and dumb craft were built to the old dimensions. They came from Watson's yard at Gainsborough, starting with the 'River' class of motor barges which acted as cargo carrying tugs. The first appeared in1929 and in 1931 they were joined by the sisters *Barlet* and *Barlock* (illustrated) with a hundred ton capacity up to Nottingham plus the craft they towed. At first they were given 90 hp Kromhout oil engines, but these were replaced by 114 hp Gardners.

Local conditions determined the shape of local craft and nowhere is this truer than in Norfolk. The rivers and broads – narrow, twisting, tidal, shallow, sometimes sheltered, sometimes exposed, demanded an adaptable craft. Originally this was the keel, a square rigged vessel but during the eighteenth century the gaff rigged wherry became more popular because she was easier to sail. Her beamy hull had a saucer shaped cross section which allowed a respectable cargo to be carried on a shallow draught, while the fine lines at bow and stern and the slipping keel gave a grip on the water, vital for successful working to windward. The single gaff sail was a triumph of ingenuity, it could be hoisted by one halliard, it could be reefed down in three stages, a bonnet could be added for extra power, and the gaff could be dropped to spill wind quickly. Without shrouds the thick counterweighted mast could be rapidly lowered for bridges by the two – speed windlass with the mate at the handle and the captain guiding the masthead onto the cabin

top. These two were all the crew and lived in the cabin aft. Sailing cargo wherries survived in decreasing numbers into the 1930s and the now restored *Albion* carried cargo into the 1960s, although today passengers replace sugar beet and bricks.

In this composition is the *Orion* of Loddon, later the *Gleaner* whose plans are at the Science Museum in South Kensington with a model at Merseyside Maritime Museum. Wherry decoration was pretty stereotyped, a black hull and a black sail, white and generally blue for the coamings, called locally the 'standing' and 'shifting right ups', red for the hatch boards, black and blue with yellow beading for the cabin panels. Many wherries had white nosings at the stem to show up at night. More variation came at the masthead where the colours were used for recognition as much as decoration. The herring hole or halliard sheave pin bearing was often garnished, where it protruded, with a star or bunch of pears device. This bunch of pears was found elsewhere, on South Wales craft for example. (see page 163)

In the picture the mastheads are from left to right: that of the *Orion* built in 1894 owned by Woods, Sadd & Moore of Loddon, millers and coal merchants; the *Albion* built in 1898 owned by W.D. & A.E. Walker, the Bungay millers; and finally the masthead of the General Steam Navigation Company who had a fleet of wherries based at Gt Yarmouth. The wind vane was elaborate, either balanced by a figure cut out of tin or a gate vane in which the tin stiffening was pierced by a star or the initial letter of the wherry's name. The figure was traditionally a Welsh girl holding a bunch of leeks – Jenny Morgan from a 19th century song, but others were used, for example Nelson at the masthead of the *Norfolk Hero*. Vane by the way was pronounced 'wain' and the attached six foot length of red bunting gave the wind strength. Names and ports of registry were painted on the panels flanking the mast tabernacle, the lettering heavily shaded and surrounded by a yellow line.

Foredeck of the restored wherry *Albion* at Coltishall in May 2001.

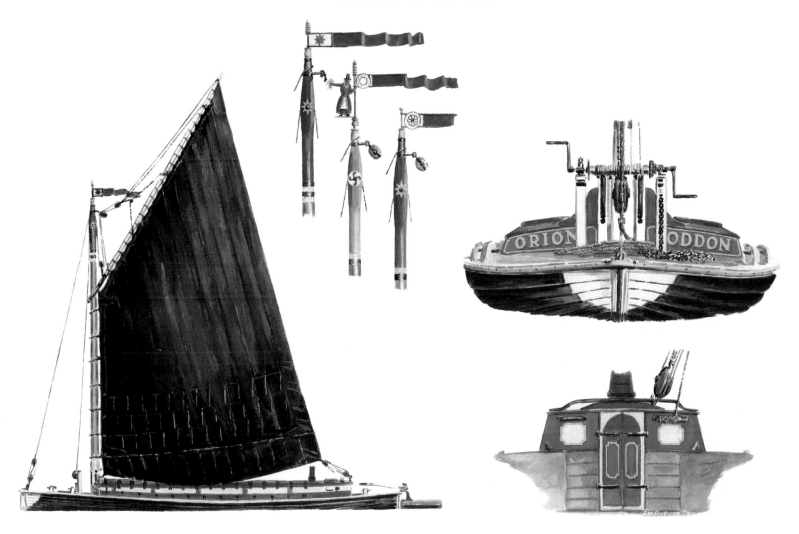

It is not known when the *Spray* was originally built but we do know that she was salvaged from the bottom of Yarmouth harbour in 1901, extensively refitted and then re-registered at Norwich in 1902. Her owner was William Royall, a member of a long established family of wherrymen, and he worked her until he retired in the 1920s. Cargoes included grain and timber but his most regular contract was delivering ice from Lowestoft to Norwich where it was used by the butchers to keep their meat fresh, and by the town morgue for its inmates. *Spray* had a black hull and white planksheers but as a high stern sheet wherry, flush decked without a cockpit to stand in, she did not carry the white quadrants on the bow, common to other wherries. The bow view shows the pivoted windlass barrel swung out of the way to allow the mast heel to come up. The vane at the masthead with its 6 foot of lightweight red bunting, so essential to the sailing master to judge the wind, had a simple S cut into the gate. William died in 1936, aged 83, and the *Spray* was soon afterwards taken to Brundall and sunk alongside so many other redundant wherries.

Albion under sail, 2001.

Although not inland craft, sailing barges did use rivers and canals. They were a big family with a maritime decorative tradition. The old Western barges which navigated the full length of the Thames and on to the Thames & Severn Canal had, one imagines, the simplest of decoration, painted washboards at the bow, painted transom, rudder post head and tiller and possibly the coloured band or bands on the sprit (pronounced spreet) which stayed as the major recognition feature of the sailing barge. Bow, quarter and transom paintwork came to be enhanced by scrollwork and chevrons, arrows and lining, cut in and painted. A selection from three sizes of barge have been illustrated, from a 'stumpy' in the river and estuary trade, from the coasting barge with a bowsprit and from her smaller sister the staysail barge without a bowsprit. Although the barge's name was generally cut in forward, on the transom it was usual to paint the name and port of registry within a scroll or garter, the name on one side, the port of registry on the other side of the stern post, with the scroll on the quarter matching that on the stem. The rest of the decoration was simply a matter of colour applied to windlass and winch, coamings, cabin top, bulwarks and gunwales as well as the topsides of the hull. Greens and blues were favoured for bulwarks, red for winches, but any house style the owner might have was not necessarily followed. The sails offered space for a badge, trade mark or advertisement.

The stumpy *Garfield* of 1882 owned by Smeed, Dean & Co, the Kentish brickmakers, carried in common with their other barges the company's triangle trade mark. This was displayed too on their 'bob' or houseflag, which stiffened by a wire frame acted as a wind vane too. R. & W. Paul, the Ipswich maltsters, distinguished their barges with a cross on the topsail which appears too on the 'bob'. Their *Ena* of 1906 is still in their ownership in the role of a director's yacht. Cranfield's, the Ipswich millers, had a white disc, while Eastwood's simply said what they did on the mainsail of the *Westmoreland*. She was built in 1900 and remained with the Eastwoods until 1963 when she was presented to the Thames Barge Sailing Club. The *Pudge* of Rochester built in 1922 is now run by the Club.

Above: Greenwich built champion Thames barge *Giralda* displaying her trophy pennants in 1900 or 1906.

Wey and Basingstoke

As offshoots of the Thames, the Wey Navigation, the Godalming Navigation and the Basingstoke Canal were improved to take Thames craft; their locks would admit barges up to 72 ft long by 13 ft 6 in wide but low water levels, particularly on the Basingstoke Canal, prevented full loads. Lightening boats were a regular feature here. Some Basingstoke barges, the 'Reso's' or residential boats, had living accommodation for captain and mate, but they were rarely family boats; the 'Odd 'Uns' were day boats and lightening craft. The *Red Jacket* illustrated was a Reso built by W.E.Costin at Berkhamsted for A. J. Harmsworth in 1911, a sister ship to the *Blue Jacket* built by Costins in 1909. Each was 72 ft by 13 ft 2 in and could carry up to 70 tons of coal on a draught of 4 ft 9 in, but nothing like this was possible on the Basingstoke. The *Red Jacket* was rebuilt at Ash Vale in the late 1920s and eventually sold in 1940 for work in the explosives traffic to and from the works at Waltham Abbey on the Lea and perished in an air raid.

Similar were the barges of the Wey Navigation of which the *Diligent* was the last to be built. She was launched at Dapdune Wharf, Guildford, in January 1940 by and for Wm Stevens & Sons, the owners and the principal carriers of the navigation. With the *Hope* and the *Perseverance IV* she carried grain to Coxes Mill at Weybridge until this traffic ceased in 1969. Stevens' barge decoration was plain, with the vessel's name shown only in the steering well although they should have had it on the transom. The number 1393 on the transom was the Port of London Authority registration number, successor to the Waterman's Hall number found on narrow boats. This was the owner's number but there was an individual boat number as well, 16049 for the *Diligent*. Because these barges were lived aboard they came under the *Canal Boats Act* for health regulations and inspection, Port of London 567 in the case of *Diligent*. If they were not registered under the *Canal Boats Acts* they came under the *Merchant Shipping Act, 1894* which demanded another official number. Because of their length, Wey and Basingstoke barges had hinged rudders which could be pulled right over in the locks. Their tillers could be angled up by means of stepped wedges so that the steerer could see over high loads such as timber. He was further helped if he used a tall 'dolly' as the tiller pin was called, 18 inches as opposed to the usual 9 inches. The little sketch shows the rig of the smaller craft which worked up the Wey onto the Wey & Arun Junction Canal and the Arun Navigation where the sprit rig was needed. They varied from 45 to 70 ft long.

River Wey barge *Reliance* about to leave Thames Lock in the 1950s, with captain Fred Legg at the tiller.

Stover Canal

The barges of the isolated Stover Canal in Devon of 1792 were never numerous for the canal was only ever two miles long. Its near neighbour the Hackney canal was even shorter, just five-eighths of a mile. The barges were wooden hulled with flat bottoms and could set a single square mainsail for use on the Teign where they were dependent on the tide. On the canal they were bow-hauled although the sail could be used in a fair wind but would have to be lowered for bridges. They were 50 foot long by 14 foot beam, designed specifically for the carriage of the local ball clay down to ships at Teignmouth where the River Teign meets the sea, although they did occasionally carry cargo upwater too: coal, timber or sand. The barges, of 25 tons capacity, were given a bluff bow, a wide square stern and a long wide hatch which could be covered by a tarpaulin. The mast was stepped in a tabernacle and was unsupported by shrouds. Whilst the Haytor Granite Tramway was in use in the early

part of the nineteenth century granite from Dartmoor was also an important traffic. Owners, mainly the clay companies, were distinguished by the colours of their barges' gunwales, white for Watts, Blake, Bearne & Co., black for the Hackney Canal Co., and green for the Devon and Courtney Clay Co. The Great Western Railway as owners of the Stover Canal also ran barges, but the main user was Watts, Blake, Bearne & Co. who latterly leased the canal and employed first a steam then a motor tug for the by now unrigged barges. By 1931, with traffic beginning to fall off, there were sixteen still in use, but all were old and in disrepair and trade finally ceased in 1942.

Above: Hackney Canal barge aground at Teignmouth at low tide, October 1937.

Left: Stover Canal barges at Teigngrace in October 1937 with the *George V* in the foreground.

Bridgwater & Taunton

Traffic on the Bridgwater & Taunton Canal and associated waterways was in the hands of barges of varied capacity, some of which were used on the lower Parrett. There seems to have been three sizes – 18 ton, 15 ton, and 5 ton 'shoes', the last exclusively canal craft, possibly going onto the Chard and Grand Western. Decoratively none of them were remarkable, but the flat bottomed clinker planked hulls were shapely and strong, designed to take the ground. The 53 ft by 13 ft 15 ton barges, among their other brickyard cargoes, loaded estuary silt to be baked into bath bricks for cleaning and scouring. Their holds were open with a small cabin forward for the two men and a cuddy aft for the equipment. Horse hauled on the canal, they depended on the tide for lower river work and were steered by 25 ft sweeps working in grooves at stem and stern. The rudder was only used on the canal or if under tow. Slowing and stopping in the tideway was done by heaving the drag chains overside. These were secured inboard but could be shortened up forward by throwing them round the 'livers', lengths of forked timber, and after by securing them to the cleats called 'clinks' and 'ballards' or bollards.

The part plan view shows the wheelbarrow planks for loading the silt at low water and unloading at the Bridgwater kilns and the four 'geds' or stakes for shafting and mooring. There was a hand net for salmon, a side industry, and a scoop for baling. Decoration was limited to a white line below the gunwale and to figures and shapes on the after bulkhead and the inboard side of the steering well. Most of the owners were brick and tile makers such

Two River Parrett barges moored at Bridgwater in Somerset sometime before 1883.

as Colthurst Symons & Co. Ltd., H. J. & C. Major and the Somerset Trading Co. Ltd., successors to John Brown, whose craft sported a lozenge, while Pocock's, barge owners and builders, favoured animal decoration such as this collie.

Canal traffic, which was mostly coal, was extinct before the 1914-18 War but carriage of silt remained until after 1945, although by that time much reduced, and there was some latter-day timber traffic within the docks. The little 17-18 ft boats carried turf and withies on the navigable drains or 'rhynes', pronounced 'rheens'.

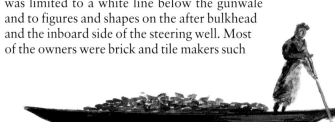

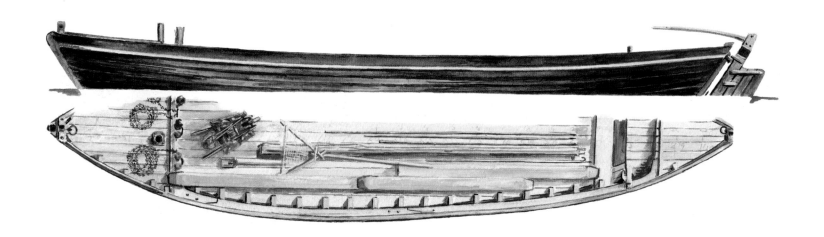

Severn and Channel

Not very colourful, but illustrating three stages in the development of Severn and Bristol Channel craft, we start with the sailing trow. Historically she was square rigged and small 50ft upriver trows survived in the trade to Ironbridge into the 1880s. By this time traffic below Stourport was in the hands of tugs and lighters and the sailing trows found work as estuary and coastal traders. By the mid-nineteenth century some were quite large, 75ft or so, and carried a ketch rig. Most trows were square sterned and often hung a pair of lifebuoys outboard.

The *Atlanta*, 143 gross tons, was built at Bristol by G.K.Stothert in 1884 and was later acquired (certainly by 1891) by the Severn & Canal Carrying Company for coastwise trade from Severn ports as far up as Worcester. Iron hulled, she was motorised in 1916 with a two cylinder Bolinder and sold in 1934 to Gilchrists for the Bristol Channel trade. By this time Severn & Canal had introduced a new breed of channel craft starting with the motor vessel *Severn Trader* built by Charles Hill at Bristol in 1932. Some of the new fleet were tankers, both powered and dumb, and construction was continued by British Waterways until the 350 ton capacity *Severn Side* was completed in 1952. The *Severn Trader*, which could carry 175 tons of cargo, has a sister still afloat as a restaurant in the Bristol City Docks.

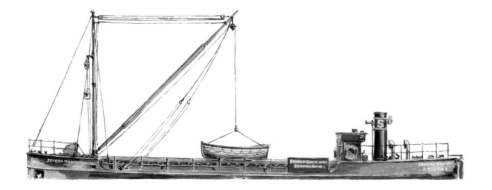

Above left: The restored Severn trow *Spry* at the Gloucester Waterways Museum in 1996.

Above right: Severn & Canal's 1932 vessel *Severn Trader* was still working under British Waterways ownership into the 1960s.

SEVERN & CANAL CARRYING CoLᴛᴰ CARRIERS BY WATER

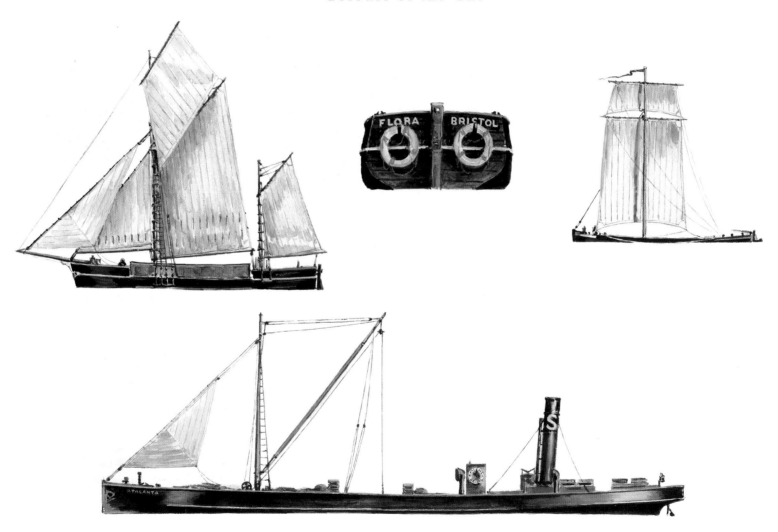

Wich Barges

One localised group of Severn trows became known as the 'Wich barges', a diminution of Droitwich. They were wooden, single masted and quite small, limited to 64 ft long by 14 ft wide by the locks of the Droitwich Canal up from the Severn, (although these were extended to narrow boat length in the 1850s when the canal was connected to the Worcester & Birmingham). The export of salt was the main traffic with coal from South Wales and The Forest of Dean inwards as back cargo. As with many other working boats under sail

coloured bands at the masthead were the distinguishing marks of different companies. The colours of the one carrying the *Rose* windvane are those of the Salt Union craft although I am unsure of the ownership of the other two. Salt acts as a good preservative for wooden hulls and it was reported that the 'wich barge' *William* was 130 years old when she was wrecked in 1939. The *Harriet* shown here was photographed at work in 1904 in Droitwich and her hull still survives as a hulk on the bank of the Severn at Purton.

Above left: The trow *William,* built in 1809, is seen here in Cumberland Basin, Bristol in May 1933.

Above right: The hulk of the *Harriet* at Purton riverbank in 1987.

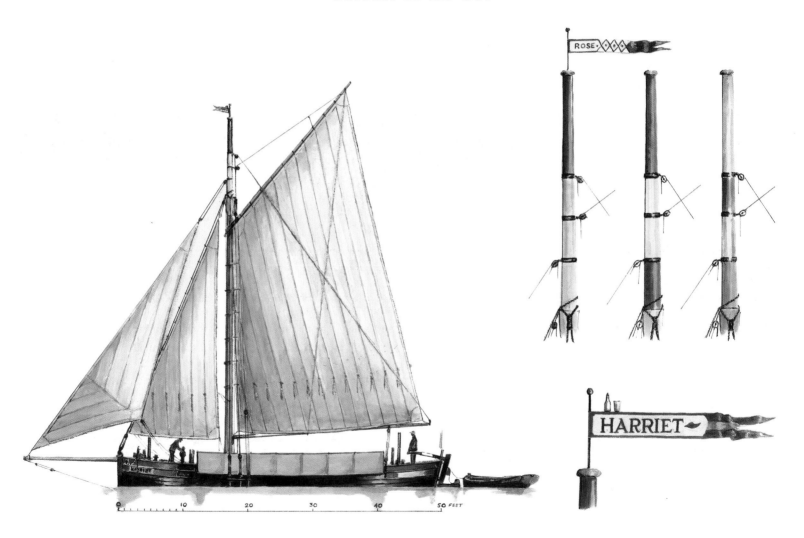

Tugs were introduced on the Severn in the 1850s and were soon to take over much of the traffic, towing rigged and unrigged trows, barges, and narrow boats. Prominent carriers were the Danks who in 1873 merged with Fellows & Co. to form the Severn & Canal Carrying, Shipping & Steam Towing Company Limited, the Fellows part of the business becoming, from 1889, a constituent of Fellows Morton & Clayton who thus gained an interest in Severn & Canal. Towage formed an important part of the latter's work and in 1886 the iron *Alert* was built for them by Finch & Co. of Chepstow. She was of particular value in Lysaght's sheet iron traffic from Wolver-hampton to Bristol, and remained in service to 1931 when diesel tugs were being introduced.

Closely linked with Severn & Canal were the towage operations of The Sharpness New Docks & Gloucester & Birmingham Navigation Company, the title since 1874 of the proprietors of the Gloucester & Berkeley Ship Canal, the new docks at Sharpness and from 1874, the Worcester & Birmingham and Droitwich Canals. There had been steam tugs on the Ship Canal since 1857, the canal's towing contractor Timothy Hadley hiring one two years later. In 1860 the new *Moss Rose* was delivered, followed by the *Mayflower* in 1861, both built by Stothert & Marten in Bristol. Many more followed, but whereas they were either scrapped or motorised, the *Mayflower* survived as a steamer proving herself in the severe winter of 1962/3 when the motor tugs had to give up. Sold for scrap in 1967, the *Mayflower* nevertheless remained afloat and was rescued in 1981 by the Bristol City Museum & Art Gallery whose team restored her.

Steam tug *Alert* in Gloucester Docks, sometime between 1909 when S.& C. C. Co. were re-formed and 1931 when she was withdrawn from service.

Canal boats in South Wales were built to different gauges, but all were shorter and wider than English narrow boats, the Glamorganshire size being some 60 ft by 8 ft 6 in carrying 20 tons on a 2 ft 9 in draught. Opened in 1794 the Glamorganshire became the preserve of its largest shareholders the Crawshays, the Merthyr ironmasters, so company carrying was an early feature. Imported iron ore up, and increasing tonnages of coal down (from the 1830s steam coal) became the traffic pattern. Eventually the railways secured most of the coal trade and the canal deteriorated, later history being punctuated by breaches, the final one at Nantgarw in 1942 closing the system except for a short length in Cardiff. One of the last boats at work was the Company's *No.451*, afloat on maintenance duties in 1943. *451* was the gauging number which acted also as a fleet number. It was painted on an iron plate nailed to a wooden board with gable shaped eaves to keep the rain off. The registration number was in Roman numerals; by the 1940s there were few boats registered.

Left & above: Glamorganshire Canal Co. boats in Cardiff in September 1936.

Whereas decoration on the Company's boats was sparse, the bye-traders or hobblers were more generous, but in a different tradition than their English counterparts. The lozenge on the top plank was found on other South Wales canals such as the Monmouthshire, while the bunch of pears device has echoes elsewhere, for example on the mast of a Norfolk sailing wherry marking the pin for the halliard sheave. Hobblers named their boats across the forward bulkhead of the cabin, the gauging number staying on the cabin side under the owner's name. Where their registration numbers went is unknown, not surprisingly since there were none after 1914 and no photographs have survived.

Mersey Flats

On Merseyside much coastal and river traffic was handled by sail up to the 1920s. Most canals had fixed bridges and there could be no sailing on them. They were the preserve of the 'cut' flats such as those owned by the Rochdale Canal Co. (see page 171) Only on the lower part of the St Helens Canal, the Weaver and Mersey & Irwell could a 'mast' flat operate. Many were built on the St Helens at Sankey Bridges by Clare & Ridgeway. One of their last was the *Eustace Carey*, 74 ft long, of 1905 for United Alkali. She was a coaster or 'outside' flat of up to 175 tons capacity, rigged as a ketch but locally called a 'jigger'. Her decoration was not striking nor was that of the probably 'inside' or river flat *Charity*, 58 ft long, 80 tons capacity of 1858 owned by James Perry of Birkenhead. Her distinguishing feature, as on most flats and on the Weaver Packets, was the painting of coloured bands at the masthead for recognition. There are models of the *Eustace Carey* and of the *Charity* at the Merseyside Maritime Museum.

Left: The 'jigger' flat *Santa Rosa* posed with all sail set at Clare & Ridgeway's yard at Sankey Bridges, near Warrington, about 1906.

Right: Typical single-masted sailing flat at work in the Mersey, probably during the 1930s.

Instant recognition was needed for the flats carrying explosives, the 'powder hoys' owned by the Liverpool Magazines Company of Bromborough. These took explosives for export from the powder hulk *Swallow* moored off Magazines Village to ships anchored in the powder grounds in the Crosby Channel, well downstream. They had four sailing flats of special construction with copper fastenings and fittings. No 1 *Bebington* was their biggest, built at Northwich in 1859, of some 60 tons capacity although only 25 tons

of explosive. The 'powder hoys' lasted under sail into the 1930s when they were unrigged. Three became dumb barges towed by the *Birkenhead* which was turned into a motor tug. All were withdrawn from service in 1945. Tanned sails were pretty well universal among the flats and their high peaked gaffs were distinctive. To ease work for the crews – two men in the river, three or four outside – the blocks were made large and mostly chain and wire running rigging was employed.

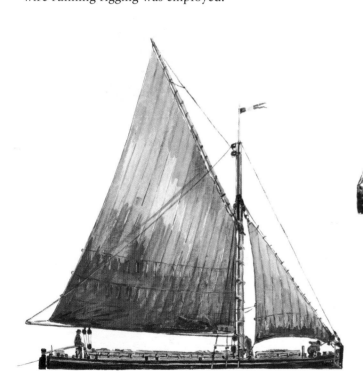

'Dukers' was the all-embracing title given to craft operated by the proprietors of the Bridgewater Canal from the third Duke of Bridgewater onwards to the Bridgewater Department of the Manchester Ship Canal Company, be they flats, floats, lighters, tugs or narrow boats. (see page 105) Here however are the craft most usually called Dukers, the flats for which the canal was built. The Duke of Bridgewater was determined to keep as much traffic as possible in his own hands and by the use of flats (he had 60 flats and 46 lighters when he died in 1803), he could offer shippers the use of vessels equally at home on the canal or the River Mersey. At first the Duke had hoped to cross the river by an aqueduct and bring his canal into Liverpool, but he found it more rewarding to allow the Trent and Mersey to join him at Preston Brook and build their line on to Runcorn. In this way he was able to control the Mersey exit of the whole Midlands network, forcing transhipment from Midlands narrow boats into his estuarial flats.

Before steam towage was introduced on the Mersey between Runcorn and Liverpool in the early 1830s, the Duke's flats would have had to hoist mast and sail for the river passage, but lower or remove them for the canal overbridges. The appearance of these early Dukers is not known for sure, not their colours or decoration. Eventually three sizes were recognized, the large Birkenhead flats which were too big to go up Runcorn locks and were not therefore canal craft, the 'Preston' flats which went as far as the transhipment wharves at Preston Brook, and the smaller Manchester flats which went the full length of the canal. Minimum dimensions were 71 feet by 14 ft 3 in, and on the canal 80 tons was possible on a 4 ft draught, with 90 tons on a 5 ft maximum draught to Preston Brook. Wooden Dukers (there were up to 490 by 1914) were universal until the 1940s. They were built at the Duke's yard at Worsley, at Stretford, and a few at the later Bridgewater Navigation Company's big repair dock at the Sprinch, Runcorn. One of these was the

Duker barges unloading imported grain at the Kelloggs' factory at Trafford Park in 1958.

Coronation, launched in the Coronation year of 1911 and in service into the 1950s. Red became the predominant decorative colour of the Dukers, coupled with yellow lettering and varnish work on the stern rail. Naming was diverse but there was a river series. The two white rings on the stove chimney, akin to the funnel colours of the Manchester Ship Canal Company, were inherited from the Duke's Trustees.

After the Second World War the Bridgewater Department modernized their fleet by ordering new steel craft from two Northwich shipyards. Three motor tugs and four power barges came from Isaac Pimblott's, whilst two power barges came from W. J. Yarwood's. Pimblott's built three dumb craft and Yarwood's sixteen.

The power barges, named with a 'Par' prefix, retained the Duker red; the *Parfield*, one of the Yarwood pair, was completed in 1952 with a 68 hp Gardner diesel, and could carry 70 tons. The motor tugs were named after local places like *Appleton* and *Faddeley*, following the fashion of the old steam tugs, while the dumb craft were named after Cheshire and Shropshire meres. The *Bigmere* was the second of the Yarwood-built dumb flats and was delivered in 1948. Later craft differed slightly and there were obvious differences between Yarwood and Pimblott vessels. These steel dukers were given a green and yellow livery and had holds protected by coamings and hatch boards. The *Bigmere*, with a capacity of 114 tons on a draught of 5 ft 6 in is preserved at the Boat Museum at Ellesmere Port.

Steam revolutionised carrying on the River Weaver. It was introduced by the Winsford salt producers led by H.E.Falk, who in 1865 built the iron *Experiment* with a capacity of some 150 tons. She was designed to tow another dumb barge laden with salt for export from Liverpool or Birkenhead. Further steam packets followed of greater capacity and power, able to tow up to three dumb craft. They drove the sailing flats either out of business or into being converted into dumb barges. Some packets were made from old iron salt pans but many were wood and some composite with iron or steel frames and wooden planking. A few had started life as sailing vessels. There were several shipyards at Winsford, some owned by the salt producers such as Falk's, others independent. With rationalisation and the formation of the Salt Union in 1888, a similar policy was applied to the Winsford yards with the former Deakin yard becoming the centre for repairs to the Salt Union packets. The *Vale Royal* had been built here in 1873 as a wooden sailing flat for George Deakin's own fleet. Converted to steam in 1883, her salt cargoes ensured longevity and she remained on the Weaver until 1936. She went then to the Mersey as a steam lighter and was not withdrawn until 1953. Note the rope fenders, the punt on the hatches and the lowered mast. The funnel lowered too because of Hartford road bridge, rebuilt in 1938, and the fixed Town Bridge at Northwich. Packets followed sailing flat tradition by having bands of colour at their mastheads for recognition purposes, red, white, red in the case of the Salt Union, while the rudder head was light blue. Machinery was usually simple expansion with two cylinders exhausting to atmosphere as in the *Vale Royal*, although some Salt Union packets had compounds and jet condensers. Boilers were return tube and usually set athwartships with the funnel on the port side, so saving space.

From 1888 Brunner-Mond were running their own steam packets, all locally built. The first was the wooden *Shamrock* built by John Woodcock at his Castle yard in Northwich, which in 1898 became

Wooden Weaver packet *Scotia* heading downriver below Hunts Lock in Northwich past the iron built *Opus* waiting to lock upriver to load salt at Winsford, 25 March 1957.

W.J.Yarwood & Sons who continued to build Weaver packets for Brunner-Mond and their successors ICI until 1947, while the other Northwich shipyard of Issac Pimblott completed the final two in 1948. Brunner packets were larger than the Salt Union craft and were given compound surface condensing engines and return tube boilers set fore and aft on the centre line, which meant that their funnels were central too. Later packets had the wheel forward of the funnel on a small bridge. The *Frances Poole* of 1923 was the last launched for Brunner-Mond, for 1926 saw the merger which created Imperial Chemical Industries. No more packets were to be built until the 1940s when Yarwood's delivered three more steamers and five motor vessels, also called packets. Whereas the *Frances Poole* could carry 235 tons of soda ash, the motor vessels could take 300. They were engined with four cylinder two stroke Crossley diesels and given a 15 cwt derrick worked by hydraulic winch. The last was the *Wincham* launched in 1948 and now at the Merseyside Maritime Museum, who have restored her to operational condition.

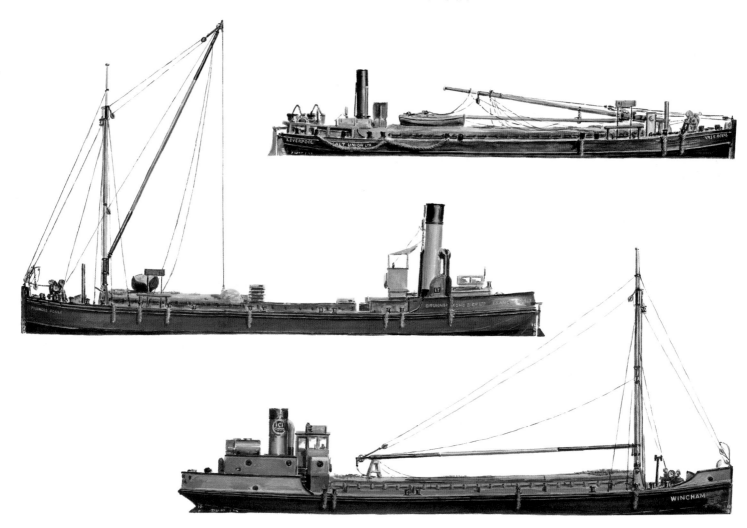

Rochdale Boats

Although the busiest of the transpennine canals, the Rochdale Canal proprietors nevertheless pursued an energetic carrying policy to maintain traffic. They had tried a carrying fleet in the very early days to gain traffic; it started in 1807 but in 1811 they gave it up because it failed to pay. They tried again in 1888 when traffic was falling off, starting with a couple of steamers, and added more, along with West Country keels small enough for the Calder and

Rochdale Canal Co. flat *Primrose* unloading cotton bales in Sowerby Bridge in June 1921.

Hebble which could offer a coast to coast service, and Mersey flats and narrow boats which could go no further east than Sowerby Bridge. Illustrated here is the flat *Primrose* in profile, one that lasted until the end of the company's carrying. Also shown is the stem of the flat *Daisy* and the stern of the West Country keel *Shamrock*.

Whereas the keels were built in the West Riding, for example at Shepley Bridge and Ledgerd Bridge near Mirfield, the flats came from Rathbones and Muggs of Stretford. All were wooden except for a final order of 18 from Yarwoods of Northwich which were wood planked on steel frames. These were built between 1906 and 1914. Flats and keels were named after flowers and the steam packets after rivers. In the end there were ten steamers and one motor boat, the *Calder*. But in 1921 like the Shropshire Union and the Leeds and Liverpool, the Rochdale gave up their fleet for the same reasons, increased costs and the unworkable eight hour day, unworkable that is unless overtime was paid, which meant more expense.

Both keels and flats depended on horses or a tow from a steam packet or a tug on the Mersey and Humber. The steam packets could manage both the Ship Canal and the Mersey. The horses hauled from a post called a neddy stepped in the lutchet which was stepped in the same position as the mast of a sailing keel, a third of the vessel's length back from the stem. The neddy could be long or short depending on the height of the load. White was the predominant colour of the Rochdale Canal Company, with blue and red embellishment, while the name and company title were cut into the top strake at stem and stern, with the name also cut into the stern rail or mainsheet horse to use the keel term. The Rochdale type of Mersey flat was closer to the keel than her Mersey estuary sister. Capacities of Rochdale flats depended on the depth of the canal, 80 to 90 tons at 5 ft draught, 50 tons at 4 ft, while West Country keels could manage 60 tons at 5 ft draught.

Steam propulsion and iron hulls came early to Scottish waterways and it was on the Forth and Clyde Canal that the puffer was born. Evolution was gradual from the steam canal scow to the coasting puffer and the pictures show some of the stages. In 1856 the Forth and Clyde horse drawn scow *Thomas* was given a steam engine; other conversions rapidly followed and by 1860 there were 25 steam vessels on the Forth and Clyde. Some of these would be new built and would have resembled the *Gartsherrie*, which was iron built for service on the Monkland Canal between Port Dundas in Glasgow, via the Cut o' Junction, and the Gartsherrie ironworks near Coatbridge. Like the Forth and Clyde, the Monkland had swing bridges so there was no height restriction. The *Gartsherrie* and a handful of others survived into the 1950s as suppliers of steam for grain elevators in Glasgow's docks. They worked for a subsidiary of the Donaldson Line and sported the company's white banded black funnel. Steam scows were simple craft, no bulwarks in way of the hold, no hatch covers, generally a vertical boiler and maybe only a single cylinder engine, although the pioneer *Thomas* had two. It was a short step to make a scow more seaworthy by providing hatch covers and allow her out onto the firths, and the canal puffers of the 1860s-70s fulfilled a dual role, being able to undertake both canal and river work, although they were allowed no further seawards than Greenock and Leith. The Carron Company of Falkirk had quite a fleet of these vessels, working between Port Dundas, the canal and the Forth ports. *No.10* here was built of iron by Barclay, Curle of Glasgow in 1871, a small product of a large shipyard. She had a vertical boiler and a two cylinder simple expansion engine. The mast and derrick were more for putting a man ashore to open bridges than to work cargo, and the mast carried the cannon ball emblem which all Carron vessels displayed.

The third vessel, the *Albert*, was built in 1886 of iron by J. & J. Hay at their Kirkintilloch yard on the Forth and Clyde for their own

fleet. She too was a canal puffer but was given bulwarks and a punt for going ashore, so she must have made some coastal passages. But she had the characteristic flush deck and low hatch coamings of the canal puffer. Her capacity was 80 tons on a seven foot draught. She was given a single cylinder engine and wheel steering more suited to coastal work than the canal puffer's tiller. Her dimensions were well within the limits of the Crinan Canal which would enable her to go up the coast and out to the inner islands such as Islay and Jura. She ended up as a coal hulk and remained afloat at Bowling into the 1950s.

Many canal puffers were, like the *Albert*, fitted with bulwarks or 'rose on' as they said. Hays built coasting puffers too at Kirkintilloch and two classes emerged, the smaller 'shorehead' boats mainly on work within the firths and the 'outside' boats which made considerable passages, across to the Antrim coast and down to Tyneside and Middlesbrough. Hays owned nearly a hundred puffers, the biggest fleet on the Clyde, and they remained in service into the 1960s under steam with the diesel ones lasting into the 1970s. Hays puffers were within the dimensions of the Forth and Clyde but other owners built bigger vessels, although all kept within the lock sizes of the Crinan Canal, so could avoid the Mull of Kintyre. The term 'puffer' referred to the original use of a non-condensing engine which simmered rather than puffed, but the name stuck and was kept into diesel days. Early puffers set sails too.

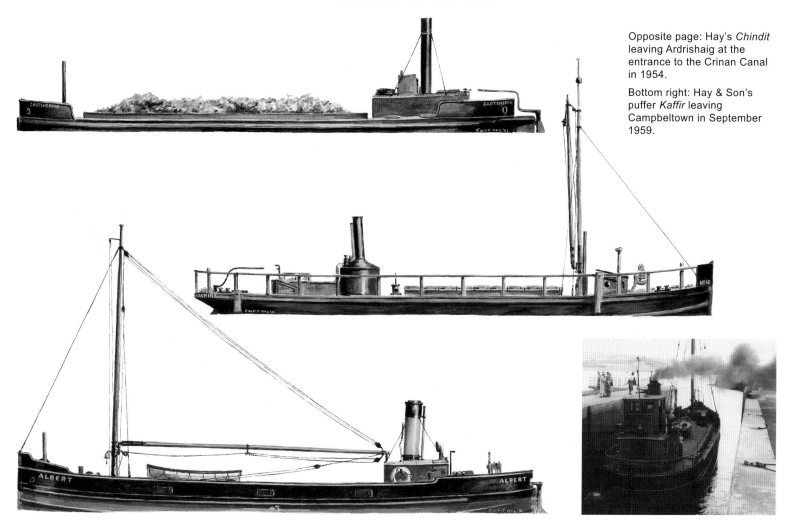

Opposite page: Hay's *Chindit* leaving Ardrishaig at the entrance to the Crinan Canal in 1954.

Bottom right: Hay & Son's puffer *Kaffir* leaving Campbeltown in September 1959.

Irish river and canal craft were not strikingly decorative. They had no outstanding features, only painted strakes and bulwark rails as on the grey Lagan lighters. Pictorial evidence is scarce except for the Grand Canal and the Barrow, which were covered by the Lawrence photographic collection. Hack boats or bye traders carried their owner's name and harbour at the stern, but boat names were not universal and many craft, certainly on the Grand, were simply numbered, like horseboat 9. Between the wars the hack boats were given numbers with a B suffix, such as *17B* to distinguish them from the Grand's fleet of M or motor boats, which started with *1M* in 1912 and ended with *79M* in 1939. Engineers' maintenance boats were given an E suffix and the G boats were the 29 wooden ones built by the Irish government during the Second War to bring turf to Dublin in case of a fuel crisis. The steel M boats built between 1925 and 1939 had no decoration apart from a red background to their number and the initials GCC, although some sported a fretted top to their stove chimney, like an early railway locomotive. *45M*, now restored, was built in Dublin by Vickers (Ireland) Ltd. in 1928. She sank at Garrykennedy on Lough Derg in 1946 but was salvaged and

Guinness barge *Killiney* on the River Liffey in the 1950s.

may now be seen up and down the Grand, although based near Robertstown. These M boats were very like Leeds and Liverpool short boats and of similar size, 60 to 61 ft long and just over 13 ft wide. M boat capacities were 45 tons on a 3 ft 9 in draught and the engines were 15 hp Bolinders. They had elaborate draught marks for gauging purposes as the picture shows.

Although they could navigate the Shannon, M boats were not happy in rough water on the loughs and often made use of the Grand Canal's cargo carrying tugs of which there were latterly three motor ones, headed by the *St James*, built in 1938 by the Liffey Dockyard in Dublin. She was 73 ft long by 14 ft 8 in beam and could carry 70 tons on a 4 ft 7 in draught. She had an 80 hp twin cylinder Bolinder. Sold in 1960 she is still in commission on the Shannon. In earlier times Grand Canal boats on the river were dependent on steam tugs introduced in 1846, while turf traffic was handled by 50 ton capacity sailing sloops, of which a couple remained in use into the 1920s.

Much of the traffic on the Grand and Shannon was porter and, on the Liffey, the Guinness brewery had their own steam barges to take shipments down to the quays below the bridges and to the docks for overseas shipment, including Scotland, England and Wales. They were introduced in 1868, at first using the Grand's Circular Line to the Liffey at Ringsend, but from 1873 they worked from Victoria Quay on the Liffey alongside the brewery. In 1927 a new design of steam barge was introduced built at the Liffey Dockyard. There were seven of them, named after local places, 79 ft long by 17 ft 6 in beam with two cylinder simple expansion engines. They could carry 90 tons on a 5 ft draught. All were withdrawn by August 1961 because of the increasing use of road transport, but the *Castleknock* and *Chapelizod* went up to Lough Neagh as sand carriers. Both funnel and crane were hinged for the Liffey bridges and the crane had its own engine. The blue hull and red funnel were the same as the Guinness steam and motor ships in the Irish Sea.

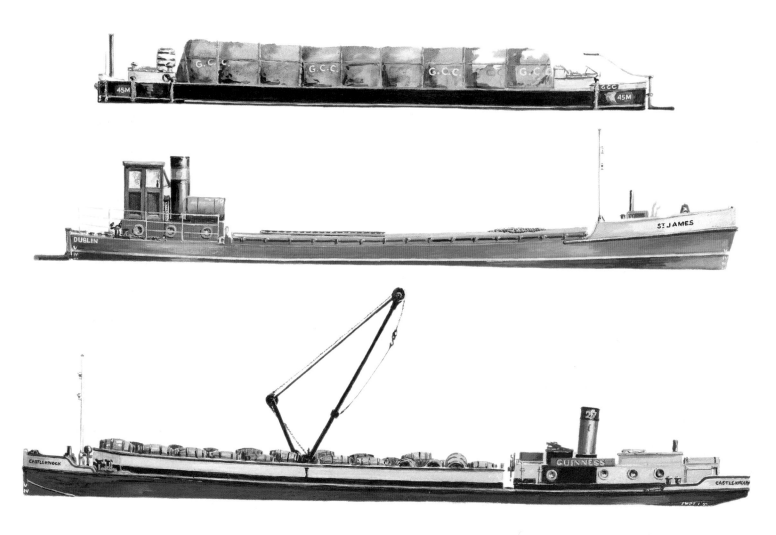

Published by

Landmark Publishing Ltd
Ashbourne Hall, Cokayne Ave
Ashbourne, Derbyshire DE6 1EJ England
Tel: (01335) 347349 Fax: (01335) 347303
e-mail: landmark@clara.net
web site: www.landmarkpublishing.co.uk

ISBN: 1-84306-145-7

© The late Edward Paget-Tomlinson, 2004

The rights of the late Edward Paget-Tomlinson as author of this work have
been asserted by Pamela Paget-Tomlinson in accordance with the Copyright,
Design and Patents Act, 1993.

All rights reserved. No part of this publication may be reproduced, stored in
a retrieval system or transmitted in any form or by any means,
electronic, mechanical, photocopying, recording or otherwise without the
prior permission of Landmark Publishing Ltd.

British Library Cataloguing in Publication Data: a catalogue record for this
book is available from the British Library.

Printed by Cromwell Press Ltd, Trowbridge, Wiltshire
Design by James Allsopp
Cover design: Tony Lewery
Reproduction by Simon Hartshorne & James Allsopp

Above: Pair of British Waterways' boats working south through Fishery
Lock on the Grand Union, April 1956.

Right: Boats waiting for orders above the Anderton Lift, October 1956.